WE DO NOT WANT THE
EARTH

WE DO NOT WANT THE EARTH

THE HISTORY OF SOUTH SHIELDS LABOUR PARTY

DAVID CLARK

1992
BEWICK PRESS
TYNE & WEAR

First published in Great Britain by
Bewick Press
132 Claremont Road
Whitley Bay
Tyne and Wear
NE26 3TX

ISBN 0-9516056-5-8

Printed and bound in Great Britain by Mayfair Print
Group, William Street, Sunderland.

CONTENTS

ILLUSTRATIONS

PREFACE

The writing of this book has been a privilege as well as a labour of love. It is my small tribute to the pioneers, who a century ago in South Shields, had the vision to establish their own political party; a party of ordinary people, for ordinary people. A party dedicated to fight for equality, freedom and justice. A party determined to represent the underprivileged and to do so independent of either of the two established political parties. It is the expression of my admiration for the Labour Party members in the town who over the years have sought to build upon these foundations. It is by their efforts and sacrifices that Labour is the principal party in South Shields. Those of us who hold political office in the town do so as a result of their foresight and dedication.

Over the years, I have met with nothing but friendship and kindness from the people of South Shields and for that I am so grateful. However, in preparing this book I am particularly indebted to the time and assistance of some of the early party activists. Ella Roberts, Ivor Richardson, Hardie Mann Blatchford Henderson and the late Lord Blyton and Maggie Sutton, have all been of tremendous help in providing personal recollections and 'colour' of those days of yester-year.

In the detailed preparation of the book, the staff of both the South Tyneside Library Service and the *Shields Gazette* have been immensely helpful. Archie Potts has guided me carefully through the pitfalls of publication and Rebecca Levene, has not only typed the manuscript but also played a vital part in the preparation of the book by her suggestions, ideas and technical know-how. I am also greatly indebted to Councillor John Temple who not only has checked the local information on my behalf during the research process but in addition was able to provide advice on pertinent local matters. His help has been invaluable.

My thanks too go to my wife and daughter, Christine and Catherine, who not only endured papers untidily lying around the home but who also read the proofs and made useful suggestions.

CHAPTER ONE

Introduction

'I do not want the earth. I only ask
That portion of its plenty which is mine.'

With those words Joe Batey, one of the earliest
Labour pioneers in South Shields, began a poem he wrote
in 1904. (1) It is difficult to think of a more appropriate
motto for the South Shields Labour Party.

The history of the first hundred years of the South
Shields Labour Party is simply the story of thousands of
ordinary men and women, over the years, working to
realise a dream. The dream of a society run on a
democratic basis of fairness, freedom and justice. They
wanted a society where ordinary working people played
their full part on school boards, boards of guardians, local
councils and in the House of Commons.

The conditions in which those early pioneers lived
were appalling. Life-expectancy was short. South Shields
had some of the worst housing conditions in the country.
Disabling and killer diseases were common. Work in the
shipyards or the coal mines was hard and uncertain. It is
a testimony of their greatness that they could lift their
aspirations above their worldly difficulties and dream of
something better.

After a century, many aspects of their dreams have
been realised. The constituency has now sent a Labour

MP to the House of Commons for almost sixty years and is regarded as one of the Party's safe seats. In 1992, 29 out of the 30 councillors on the Borough Council are Labour. But that record did not simply happen. It came about because it was worked for. The propaganda meeting in the market place on a Sunday evening, the May Day rally on the sea-front, a jumble-sale here and a sale-of-work there, canvassing in the rain or snow, traipsing home along a dimly-lit street after a ward meeting or standing on a polling station on an election day, together make up part of that work.

Many of the social improvements the pioneers dreamt of have come about as a result of the policies of their Labour councils and governments. The National Health Service introduced by Nye Bevan in 1948 has done so much to wipe out the killer diseases. The Education Act of 1944 providing educational opportunity for all youngsters was to a great extent the result of the work of their own MP, J Chuter Ede. The fine housing-stock is a legacy of the work of Labour councillors over the years.

Their trust in democracy has served them well and society is so different from that of a century ago. Much, however, remains to be done as we enter our second century.

South Shields is not one of those 'special' constituencies which has experienced 'crucial' or 'historic' by-elections. Yet it has thrown up exciting characters giving proof to the old adage that real life is far stranger than fiction. One of the earliest councillors, who went on to become mayor and a respected civic figure, was involved in a gun-running plot to get arms into Russia. The anti-Labour MP immediately following the First World War was mixed-up with unsavoury characters and was himself a member of the secret service - a spy. A three-

THE PLEA OF LABOUR.

I do not want the earth. I only ask
    That portion of its plenty which is mine ;
    That I may live the life which God's design
Marked not for slothful ease or endless task.
I will not fawn at fortune's feet, nor bask
    Contented where reflected glories shine,
    Until the coming day when wrath divine
Shall tear away from Mammon's face the mask.
Give me fair recompense for dangers faced :
    Give me but fair reward for labour done ;
    A chance to breathe of God's pure air a breath
And time for rest in all the hours of haste,
    That I may see the smiling of the sun
    Ere darkness cometh in the guise of death.

The Plea of Labour by Joe Batey, 1904.

time Labour parliamentary candidate supplied explosives to a suffragette who planned to blow-up Durham Cathedral. An Independent mayor travelled to London to negotiate a large land deal only to end up buying it himself before being forced to resign in disgrace.

But there was something special about the people of Tyneside and Wearside. The appalling conditions in which they lived did much to determine their attitude to life. Perhaps the South Shields born and bred author, Catherine Cookson, who became one of the most popular English writers of fiction, captured most accurately how the local people saw themselves in the early years of the century when she wrote:

> '...the character of the people; the fact that work was their life's blood; their patience in the face of poverty; their perseverance that gave them the will to hang on; their kindness; their open-handedness; their narrowness; their bigotry, for there were those who couldn't see beyond the confines of the county of Durham, in fact little beyond Shields and Jarrow: to many a Shields man, a Sunderland man was an enemy; and, as I brought out in *Pure as the Lily*, a North Shields man would treat a South Shields man as a poaching foreigner should he cross the river to look for work...And the women. Stoics would be a better name to give to the females of that time, my early time, because for most of them along those river banks it was grind in one way or another from Monday morning till Sunday night.' (2)

The first century of Labour in South Shields is a testimony to the foresight of the early pioneers who set about the task of building a better society. There were no famous people but certainly there were strong personalities full of pluck and determination. It is simply the story of everyday folk determining their own destiny.

CHAPTER TWO

The Beginnings: 1892-1917

The Boundary Commissioners who in 1832 recommended that South Shields should have its own MP began their submission, 'Although the appearance of South Shields has little to recommend it, and its buildings are far from imposing, yet it is a place of very great importance'. That importance was economic, as the town occupied the south bank of the River Tyne and offered deep water berths.

Since then, South Shields has returned 12 MPs in its 160 years as a constituency. In doing so, it has created a record in being the only one which has been sending an MP to Westminster since 1832 and has yet to elect a Conservative MP. For most of the first 100 years of the constituency's existence, nine Liberals represented the town, and since then three Labour Members; J Chuter Ede, Arthur Blenkinsop and David Clark. South Shields can truly claim to be a radical town.

It has long been a working-class town inhabited by shipyard workers, engineering workers and miners in the three collieries of St Hilda, Harton and Marsden; the latter with a reputation for radicalism. To these have to be added the thousands of heavy industrial workers as well as the many men employed in the merchant navy. Furthermore, these were augmented by a sizable middle-class taking advantage of the seaside environs and the fashionable Westoe Village.

The miners in the town had been active in forming a union from the early industrial days. On the repeal of the infamous anti-trade union Combination Acts, they unsuccessfully went on strike in 1826 and formed the Association of Colliers on the Rivers Tyne and Wear. The main issues on which they campaigned were the annual bond, fines by employers, low wages and the truck-shops. Later, in 1831, when Tommy Hepburn formed his miners union, the Shieldsmen were active in this new body.

As early as 1872 a trades council was formed in the town, the first such permanent body in the North East of England. It survives to the present day and has continued to be in the vanguard of many progressive causes. Indeed, it was the existence of this formal working-class organisation which largely determined the course of local Labour politics in the final decade of the nineteenth century. Ironically, though, it was to act as a brake on the full development of independent representation of labour in the town.

The last quarter of the 19th Century had seen the growth of the demand from workingmen for representation on elected public bodies. This was well understood by the Liberals both locally and nationally and was especially significant in the coalfields where miners, living in concentrated communities, could offer many votes.

In the North East coalfield, the Liberals gave seats to the miners leaders. Thomas Burt was elected for Morpeth as early as 1874 and he was followed in 1885 by the election of two agents of the Durham Miners Association (DMA): William Crawford in Mid-Durham and John Wilson in Houghton-le-Spring. As elsewhere in England, the miners were very much in the fore of the Lib-Lab tradition. In South Shields this was developed through the Trades Council which had come to an arrangement with the Liberals. By 1892, there were several workingmen sitting on the Borough Council.

The Liberals in South Shields were adept at absorbing representatives of labour into their ranks without conceding any real power. For example, at the town's Liberal AGM in March 1892, there were three working-class councillors present in addition to the secretary of the Trades Council, the president of St Hilda's Miners Lodge and representatives officially appointed from the coopers and the seamens unions. Even 25 years later, Bill Blyton recalled that many of the Harton Lodge committee men were still Liberals, as indeed were his own parents until they were converted to Labour in the 1920s.

In 1891, the Harton Coal Company came about as a result of an amalgamation incorporating four collieries; St Hilda in the town centre, Harton two miles further south, Marsden (alternatively called Whitburn) three miles southerly along the coast and Boldon four miles to the south west. Many of the miners in the last three collieries lived in the centre of South Shields and had to travel to the mines. However, in the case of Boldon, most miners lived in the pit-village.

One means of travel is worthy of mention in passing - a train colloquially known as the 'Marsden Rattler'. This went along a three mile stretch of railway running from Westoe Lane Station in the town to the colliery, much of the journey being along the cliff-tops. It carried not only the miners but also ordinary passengers and coal. The return second-class fare remained 4d from the service's inception until its withdrawal on 23 November 1953. Because it was owned by the National Coal Board which was created before British Rail, it was the first passenger railway to be nationalised in Britain on 1 January 1947.

When the colliery closed in June 1968 the line ceased to be used.

In 1892, the alliance of workingmen with the Liberals was already under challenge at both the national and local level. The annual meeting of the Trades Union Congress at nearby Newcastle in September 1891 stimulated interest in alternative representation of labour. There was even speculation in the north-east regional press that Keir Hardie would contest Newcastle at the 1892 General Election.

Initially, the demand was simply for the representation of working-people. The next stage of development was for representation separate from and independent of either of the two main parties which inevitably meant an Independent Labour Party (ILP). Only after the independence had been achieved could the word independent be dropped from the Party's name. In South Shields in 1892, the demand was for an ILP.

Even as late as 1929, the local Party's political objects were described in its constitution as:

'To secure the election and maintenance of independent representatives of the industrial classes upon any elective local administrative bodies, and in the House of Commons, and also in conjunction with the National Labour Party, the ultimate formation of a united Working Class Party whose aim shall be the complete economic emancipation of the Working Classes.'

Thus the philosophic aspect of the Party's programme was left vague and merely in an unwritten form reflected the national Party's position.

However, socialist ideas were being promoted and were gaining ground with many young people. William Morris had spent some time in Northumberland and Tyneside in 1887 espousing socialist ideals. H H Champion was also active in Newcastle in the early 1890s promoting his brand of independent Labour representation which was based on anti-Liberalism and has been described as 'Tory-socialist'. In August 1890, the *Workman's Times* was launched and in December 1891 Robert Blatchford's *Clarion* was published for the first time. These two newspapers proved very quickly to be most influential in radical working-class circles.

Already Independent Labour Parties had been formed in Bradford, Colne Valley, Manchester and other parts of Lancashire and Yorkshire since the summer of 1891. This movement was spreading but Tyneside, with its strong trade union presence, initially did not respond.

However, December 1891 saw a letter in the *Shields Gazette* raising the possibility of a Labour candidate contesting the 1892 General Election in South Shields. This possibility continued to be discussed, and in April 1892, the same newspaper published a leader decrying the notion of Independent Labour Representation. (1) The following month, both the Jarrow and South Shields Trades Councils debated the issue, with the former body rejecting it by 19-9 and their South Shields counterparts deciding to let the matter lie on the table.

The discussion was taking place against the background of a miners' strike in the Durham coalfield. This added a greater poignancy and urgency to the issue. It was a bitter strike which closed every pit in County Durham but which saw all the pits elsewhere in the country working. Jack Lawson, later to be a Labour Cabinet minister, was living at neighbouring Boldon

Colliery at the time of the dispute and it remained etched on his mind . In his autobiography, *A Man's Life*, written 40 years later, he described it in these graphic terms:

> 'A national strike is a calamity, and arouses strong feelings, but a county strike is savagely bitter because its effects are more directly devastating. At any rate, in a national strike the world knows and cares a little, but in that 1892 strike, isolated, with the rest of the coalfields in full swing, it seemed as though we were forsaken and forgotten by God and man...I had even as a boy of eleven become class-conscious.' (2)

Thus in South Shields many miners must have felt as Jack Lawson did and begun to question the idea of representation through the Liberal Party. No doubt this fear figured prominently in the mind of the editor of the *Shields Gazette* when he wrote the leading article.

The Liberals were certainly aware of the threat and convened a special meeting at which a rising young miner from St Hilda Colliery, Joe Batey, firmly supported their cause by declaring that they 'had to support the Liberals for they had given workingmen the vote. To vote for any other would be base ingratitude.' (3)

It must be remembered that Batey worked at St Hilda, which was probably the most politically reactionary of the town's three pits and whose president and Lodge committee were declared Liberals. Batey was soon to change his mind and went on to play a sterling role in the emergence of the Labour Party in South Shields and beyond.

Joe Batey had been born at Killingworth, Northumberland, in 1867 and went down West Moor

Durham Miners' Wages

The Present System Condemned.

The Need for a Minimum Wage.

By J. BATEY t. Hilda Colliery, So. Shields

E. SWORD, LAYGATE PRINTING W

ONE PENNY EACH.

Joe Batey's Pamphlet, 1904.

Colliery as a trapper lad when he was 12. He moved to Blaydon as a hewer when he was 18 and when that pit closed he moved to St Hilda, becoming active in the Lodge there. He was elected checkweighman in 1896. For eighteen years he was president of St Hilda's Lodge and became a full time agent of the Durham Miners Association (DMA). In 1922 he successfully contested Spennymoor for Labour and represented that constituency until retiring in 1942 when he returned to live in South Shields. The Batey lineage continued to be strong in local Labour circles with Stella Lloyd, a niece, being a prominent councillor, another niece, Ella Roberts being a stalwart of the Women's Section for 60 years and more recently Lilian Jordison, Stella's daughter, who sat as a councillor for over 20 years. In turn, her own daughter, Lilian Malcolm, continues the family tradition as a Party member and worker.

But in spring 1892, Joe Batey no doubt reflected the consensus among rising young miners at St Hilda Colliery. This mood was, however, in a state of flux.

In March 1892, steps had been taken to establish a Fabian Society in the town and this body was also an advocate of an independent Labour Party. Many of these early adherents locally were also founders of the ILP. For example, Joe Abbott, one of the first presidents of the local ILP, was the secretary of the South Shields Fabians. At the beginning of May 1892, Katherine St John Conway, a prominent proponent of independent Labour politics and a Fabian lecturer, spoke in South Shields on 'Wealth and Work'.

Shortly after this, on 25 May 1892, with a General Election looming, the local Fabian Society members debated amongst themselves as to how they should exercise their votes. With no prospect of a Labour candidate, they decided to endorse publicly the sitting Liberal MP, James C Stevenson. He had, in line with mainstream Liberal opinion, expressed his support for a general programme of practical reforms - the so-called Newcastle programme. This had been adopted at the Liberal Party's conference in the Tyneside city in 1891 in an attempt to head-off the increasing demands for Labour representation.

Stevenson was also to emphasise his party's commitment to Home Rule for Ireland which stood him in good stead with the sizeable Irish vote in South Shields. In 1885, the *Newcastle Daily Chronicle* estimated that ten per cent of South Shields voters were Irish. In particular, this was important amongst the miners of St Hilda Colliery, many of whom were either Irish or of Irish extraction. Ivor Richardson, a Party member for over sixty years, recalls that his grandfather, Matthew Richardson, was a hewer at St Hilda in the 1890s and handled the wages for his 'marrers' or workmates. When at the weekend he went to share out the money with them at the Cyprus Hotel at Chichester, the general mode of language was Gaelic.

No Labour candidate appeared in the 1892 General Election but the debate on the representation of Labour continued unabated throughout the July election period. Indeed, the heightened interest in politics only served to fan the flames for a radical change. Doubtless as the *Shields Gazette* of 5 July reported that Keir Hardie had been elected at West Ham as the first independent Labour MP, interest in the notion of Labour representation grew. Even more so when John Barnes followed him at Battersea and Havelock Wilson in Middlesbrough.

Meanwhile, a Yorkshire-based weekly newspaper, the *Workman's Times*, began a campaign for Labour representation and throughout June and July invited those interested to write to the editor. As a result, a good number of South Shields residents replied intimating that they supported the idea. Perhaps the key which unlocked this nascent support came when Charles H Reynolds of Hull had a letter published in the paper offering 'to do a month's tour for the ILP' on Tyneside. (4)

The pressure locally for an independent Labour Party was becoming unstoppable. On 7 August a meeting was called at the Alhambra Temperance Hall at the Mill Dam in the town which demanded the state payment of MPs - a logical prerequisite for the representation of workingmen. A number of those present were soon to emerge as pioneers in the South Shields Labour Party including Joe Abbott and C H Reynolds. In essence, this was the first meeting fronted by the embryonic local Party.

Reynolds was to remain in South Shields for a number of years, eventually being elected onto the local School Board in 1896. He had immense organising ability and was without doubt the prime mover in the successful establishment of an ILP in South Shields - one of the earliest in the North East of England.

Following the success of the Alhambra meeting, the proponents of an ILP in South Shields held a series of informal meetings laying the groundwork for the formal establishment of the new party. This then took place on 31 August 1892. Not only did they establish the Party but also, in the time-honoured tradition of Labour Parties ever since, passed a resolution.

The *Shields Gazette* reported the meeting, whose consequences would revolutionise the political scene in the town over the ensuing hundred years and beyond, in the following single paragraph:

'A meeting was held last night in Brown's Cocoa Rooms, Church Way, South Shields for the purpose of forming a South Shields Branch of the National Independent Labour Party.   There was a large attendance. Mr W Willimont opened the proceedings by stating that he considered the time opportune for the formation of a Labour Party in South Shields. The following were elected as officers: Gordon Scott, President; C Richardson and R Brown, Vice Presidents; Walter Willimont and C Reynolds, Secretaries; Mr Skelton, Treasurer; and Messrs Marshall, Walker, Lawson, Clydesdale as the committee.   The following resolution was carried unanimously: "That this meeting of the Labour Party strongly condemn the action of the Master Tailors, and advise their fellow workers to abstain from purchasing from the shops where the men are locked out".'(5)

Within a few days of its inception, the new Party was able to attract over 4000 people to an open-air meeting in the market-place. It had truly caught the imagination of the age and the need for political change. This mood was infectious and shortly afterwards similar parties were formed elsewhere in the North East.

This activity could not be ignored by the Trades Council for many of its younger members were attracted by the new political force. In August 1892, it had again discussed the ILP and once more rejected the notion. The majority still preferred the cosy relationship with the established Liberal Party.

By mid-September, Reynolds was reporting in the *Workman's Times* that the South Shields ILP had almost 100 paid-up members and was still meeting every Friday at Brown's Cocoa Rooms. This was to be its temporary home until the Party moved to its own Labour Hall in Chapter Row. That the Fabian Society used the same venue for their meetings demonstrated both the closeness of the two bodies and the presence of a sympathetic landlord.

One of the problems facing such bodies as the local ILP was finding premises where they could meet. Landlords, perhaps not surprisingly, were loath to help an organisation which might turn against them politically. Such was the case in South Shields as Reynolds outlined in a letter to the *Workman's Times* on 17 September 1892.

'A committee was appointed to secure, if possible, the Central Hall, Chapter Row, for the use of the party. The person who lets the Hall is rather hard upon us, for although we offered him one quarter's rent in advance he wants some responsible person to stand as guarantor for the first year's rent. In spite of our efforts we are up to the present unable to get the guarantee.'

Reynolds' candid letter highlights the very practical difficulties the local Party had to face when it had no money and no prominent supporters either as individuals or as a corporate body such as a trade union. Brown's Cocoa Rooms were to remain the Party's headquarters for several years but the Party members were not dismayed by these difficulties and they pressed on with their beliefs and objectives.

The same letter goes on to graphically capture the mood and nature of the new party's pioneers:

'Our branch consists of young fellows with plenty of go in them...we already have several women, chiefly wives of our male members, joining the society...'

A further glimpse of the nature of the local party is gleaned from a letter in the *Workman's Times* on 1 October 1892 when a supporter laments the inactivity of the ILP in Newcastle and continues:

'In South Shields, on the contrary, the members turn-up, every week in large numbers and take part in the proceedings...One thing I was particularly pleased to see, and that was about six lady members present. Fie Newcastle what are you doing to let South Shields get ahead of you. One of the ladies took part in the discussion, speaking for a few moments in a very sensible and ladylike way. Mrs Harris (Harrison) knew how to express her thoughts clearly and fully in a few words, and when she gains more confidence, it will be a real pleasure to listen to her.'

The latter part of the letter may appear as somewhat condescending a hundred years later but clearly at the time it was a compliment not only to the woman member in particular but also to the South Shields Party in general.

Gordon Scott, who had been elected the first president, occupied the role for less than a month before standing down in late September to become correspondence secretary with Joe Abbott becoming president and Charles Reynolds being officially designated, organiser.

A deputation was received from the South Shields branch of the Fabian Society which had been formed only just before the ILP. It was agreed to co-sponsor a meeting to be addressed by the future Labour Prime Minister, J Ramsay MacDonald. This meeting was held at the Alhambra Theatre on 7 October 1892 and was adjudged a great success, with 'no opposition taking place'.

In those days, the municipal elections were held in November and the new Party was anxious to be involved. Undeterred by the initial hostility of the Trades Council, meetings were held with them to discuss joint candidates on 20 and 27 September. This was a recognition of the fact that by opposing each other, both parties would be losers and illustrated the pragmatic approach of the new ILP. They wished to be more than a political debating society and worked from the very outset to gain elected office for their members.

Their pragmatism paid off for, surprisingly, the Trades Council found one of the ILP nominees, John Lisle, to be acceptable to them. Lisle, a tailor by occupation, was an officer of the Trades Council and was likely to have been involved in the lock-out referred to at the inaugural meeting of the ILP. The result was that he won one of the seats in the Laygate Ward as a Labour candidate whilst the other Trades Council member, who ran under Liberal designation, was defeated. The new party now had a foothold on the Borough Council within 3 months of its inception.

Encouraged by such success, it grew from strength to strength. Regular meetings were held and on 15 December 1892, Katherine St John Conway paid a return visit to the town for a very successful public meeting. She had been appointed to the steering committee for a conference to be held the following month to establish an

ILP nationally and used this opportunity to urge the Tyneside pioneers to attend the Conference.

She was successful. The Conference had been called at Bradford on 13 and 14 January 1893 and Charles Reynolds was sent as delegate from the South Shields Party whilst his wife Margaret was present from the local Fabian Society. Both spoke at the Conference with the Shields organiser arguing for more representation of the northern counties on the new party's ruling body, the National Administrative Council.

On 11 February 1893, the ILP in South Shields held its first AGM and elected the following officers;

President	C H Reynolds
Vice Presidents	C Richardson
	H Smith
Secretary	W Willimont
Correspondence Sec.	G Scott
Treasurer	Mr Briggs
Committee	Mrs Reynolds, G Smith,
	R Brown, S Finnerly,
	E Hindmarsh

Such was the confidence of those present that they decided to build upon their election success and establish a second branch in the town in Tyne Dock where there was a preponderance of dockers and railwaymen. This move was to prove to be somewhat premature but it illustrated local feeling.

As the year developed, the leadership role of the Reynolds became even more apparent. He gave lectures throughout the Borough on such topics as 'What retards the Labour Movement', 'Man's Individual Responsibility', 'Why Women should join the ILP' and 'The aims and objects of the ILP'. His wife Margaret also continued to play an active part in the South Shields Party which was to culminate in her being elected the secretary in 1895. Theirs was a real partnership for Labour.

Meanwhile, in South Shields the Liberals were increasingly becoming concerned about the threat of the new organisation. Clearly it was not 'simply going to go away' as they had originally hoped. In February 1893, they decided to establish a front organisation, the Radical Association, which they hoped would prove an alternative political attraction for workingmen. This initially met with some success in attracting a few trade unionists, including Joe Batey, but it was not long-lasting. In spring 1894, this battle for the minds of young radicals was heightened when the general secretary of the national ILP, the famous trade union leader, Tom Mann, addressed a meeting in South Shields which he himself later described as being 'magnificent'.

Mann's visit spurred on the local activists. They renewed their attack on the Liberals, but it was an uphill struggle. In May 1894, there was a report in the *Labour Leader*, the national newspaper of the ILP, which highlighted some of the difficulties:

'The Trades Council is doing some good organising and educational work but little seems to be done to carry out the resolve of the Council to run a Labour man for Parliament. There has been a little friction because of the fact that the secretary of the Council is also secretary of the Liberal Association.' (6)

By August, the same newspaper was reporting further activity with a huge meeting of the ILP in the Market Place:

'Close on 3000 were present. The political position in South Shields came in for a full share of attention and some gentlemen...advocated a policy of smashing the Liberal Party. All the speakers urged those present not to support any save an ILP candidate, and the crowd responded enthusiastically. The South Shields ILP should apply to the NAC for some advice on the local situation. There is an opening for a good ILP candidate.' (7)

In the November 1894 municipal elections, the Radical Association ran candidates jointly with the Liberals including Joe Batey who was defeated at Laygate by the ILP candidate, a fellow miner, Jack Cullen who worked at Marsden. Batey soon saw the error of his ways, however, and the following month he was elected onto the Board of Guardians with the support of the ILP whom he then promptly joined.

Cullen's success meant that the ILP formally had three members on the Borough Council as Joe Abbott, a small shop keeper and former sailor, had joined Lisle in the previous year's elections at Tyne Dock. Furthermore, John Thompson, a miner, had gained a seat in Laygate and consistently supported the ILP.

John Thompson was a particularly valuable recruit to Labour's ranks. Born in 1859, he was the highly-respected leader of the Marsden miners, being both their checkweighman and lodge secretary from the 1880s. He was a self-educated man to whom the whole mining community turned for advice and counsel. In 1921, the lodge members did him the great honour of having his portrait featured on their banner and when he died in the midst of the great miners' strike, many thousands lined the streets in respect for his funeral cortege on 20

John Thompson's portrait on Marsden Lodge Banner, 1921.

December 1926. He sat on the council for Laygate from 1893 to 1896 and for the Westoe Ward from 1898 until 1907. John Thompson epitomised all that was good within the mining community. He valued education and sought to improve himself in this respect, was regarded as completely incorruptible and honest and as someone whose judgement was always sound. He was truly the pillar of the Marsden mining fraternity.

In 1895, the ILP's first councillor, John Lisle, lost his seat in Laygate. The ILP itself may have been partly responsible for this loss. The ward was a two-member one and they approached the Trades Council seeking endorsement for Charles Reynolds in addition to Lisle himself. There was no difficulty with Lisle, but in spite of Reynolds being supported by the Plasterers Union to which he belonged, the Trades Council refused endorsement arguing that as he was being run by the ILP 'they could not support him because the Council had nothing to do with politics.' (8) That they did in fact back Lisle again suggests that this reason was somewhat hollow. Reynolds contested the ward alongside Lisle but the result was that a Conservative and a Liberal were elected. Nothing more was heard of John Lisle, but he can legitimately claim to have been elected as the first independent Labour councillor on South Shields Borough Council. The following year, however, saw Joe Abbott retain his seat whilst Joe Batey was returned in Laygate for the ILP. Meanwhile Charles Reynolds, having unsuccessfully contested the municipal elections on a number of occasions, was elected onto the School Board.

Thus the local Party had survived its tempestuous birth. Although the party activists did not contest the 1895 General Election they had achieved considerable success in their first four years. Not only had they fought off concerted attacks from both the Liberal Party and the

Trades Council but they had achieved representation of their members on various elected bodies. Their president, Charles Reynolds, sat on the School Board, Joe Batey on the Board of Guardians and three of their number sat on the town council They could look back on their initial foray into local politics with pride and satisfaction.

Following this successful period, a time of consolidation took place. The ILP nationally went through a difficult phase and this was reflected locally with both Abbott and Batey losing their seats in 1899. The early pioneers were not downcast and they continued to campaign for their beliefs. One of the difficulties they faced, was the plethora of bodies competing for the working-class votes. The Liberals, either directly through front organisations, or in coalition with the Trades Council, fought to retain their political hold.

Added to this was the popularity of the sitting Liberal MP, W S Robson. He was a radical lawyer who took an interest in industrial legislation and who in 1899 piloted through the Commons the progressive Education (Half-Timers) Act which raised the school leaving age from 11 to 12. Robson also built up a following with the unions and in 1900 the Marsden Lodge of the DMA had his portrait painted onto their banner.

But in the mid-1890s, the Liberals were secretly very nervous about the new Party's success and none more so than the MP. He had previously lost his Middlesbrough constituency in 1892 to a Labour candidate, J Havelock Wilson, who by a strange quirk of fate would go on to become the anti-Labour MP for South Shields in 1918. In October 1896, Robson wrote to his wife the following:

'At a meeting of pitmen the other day, a circular from some trade organisation was submitted

containing a clause that the miners should only vote
for Labour candidates at the next election. This was
promptly scouted and Bransby [his agent] says he
doesn't believe there is a single miner who will vote
against me. Bransby also says that in his calls
everybody has borne testimony to my popularity
with all classes. That is my sheet anchor.
Liberalism apart from the claims or personality of a
Liberal candidate seems to have a very thin thread
of life here.' (9)

Robson showed he was acutely aware of the threat of
Labour. He seemed to believe that the Liberal hold on the
town was weakening and that their time was limited.

On the other hand, the local ILP also faced
competition from another quarter, the presence of an
alternative socialist body, a branch of the Social
Democratic Federation (SDF) which was formed in 1904.
The leading figure in that body was Jimmy Dunlop who
from 1904 consistently fought local elections, splitting
the ILP vote. Prior to forming a local branch of the SDF, he
had been active in the South Shields ILP and as its
delegate had attended the annual conference of the
national body in 1900. However, he found the politics of
the ILP a little tame for his liking. He was a colourful and
fiery character who eventually became a Labour councillor
for Tyne Dock in 1906, an alderman in 1918 and also an
early Labour mayor in 1928-9.

Dunlop was on one occasion arrested by the police on
suspicion of gun-running. Following the abortive
revolution to overthrow the Tsarist Regime in Russia in
1905 led by Father Gapon, there were various attempts to
smuggle arms there. The Tyne with its direct and regular
links to the Baltic in general, and St Petersburg in

particular, was an obvious place from which to despatch the arms.

In the spring of 1907, there were other arrests on Tyneside and Wearside which culminated in convictions in April and May. Dunlop himself was not charged but when the police searched his home they found a broken box in the cellar which they suspected had held munitions. On the box they discovered an address in Edinburgh which allowed them to trace the ringleaders in the gun-running organisation. The police thus felt satisfied, foregoing a trial, and the recently elected councillor escaped the infamy of going to court.

The problems of the local Party were further exacerbated in the early 1900s when their leader, Charles Reynolds, left the town to move to Whitby where he continued to be active in Labour politics whilst running a boarding-house.

At the turn of the century, the Labour leaders were beginning to realise that some accommodation had to be made with the Trades Council and later the SDF if they were to continue to make inroads at municipal elections. In 1902, the ILP wrote to the national Labour Representation Council (LRC), which had been formed in 1900. They sought advice on how a local LRC could be established to coordinate electoral activity. As a result the LRC approached the South Shields Trades Council but was initially rebuffed. However, by 1905, a local LRC was established but with limited success, mainly cooperation between the SDF and the ILP.

It is not without significance, that a number of these early Labour councillors described themselves as checkweighmen, for this position had a very special place in the miners' life. Miners in those days were paid by results - by the amount of coal hewed and tubs filled. In order to ensure that the mining companies paid the full amount due and did not cheat, the miners elected from amongst their own number, the checkweighman, whose task was literally to check the weight of coal won. It was obviously a crucial position. They had to be above being bought by the mining companies. Thus those elected were the most respected, trustworthy and honest members of the mining community. Inevitably, these men were natural leaders and that they became converts to Labour's ranks was vital to any electoral breakthrough. In South Shields, Joe Batey and John Toll were checkweighmen at St Hilda whilst John Thompson and Richard Vine occupied the same role at Marsden and Harton respectively. All four were highly regarded Labour councillors before 1910.

Prior to 1905, the Labour stalwarts had been reduced to three councillors; Batey, Cullen and Thompson. Following the establishment of the LRC in 1905, Robert Hearn, a member of the ILP was elected. In 1906 John R Toll and Jimmy Dunlop joined him and they in turn were followed by Richard Vine in 1907. Thus the fight back by the Liberals in the first few years of the 1900s had been challenged but it was some time yet before the Party made the crucial breakthrough into the majority position. However, by 1907 there were six bona-fide Labour councillors on the local authority.

But Labour's growing cohesion, although far from perfect, was beginning to have a political impact in the town. The Liberal MP, W S Robson, was becoming most concerned at its advance. His biographer wrote:

'In South Shields Robson was increasingly experiencing pressure from the Left, although no Labour candidate was ever put in the field against him. The pressure from Labour from 1900 onwards was unmistakeably increasing, and much of Robson's effort in his constituency was devoted to showing that in the sphere of social reform, Liberalism could offer as much as Labour.' (10)

Clearly, to judge by the reactions of these opponents, the Labour activists were making progress.

During 1907 Philip Snowden MP visited South Shields, attracting a huge crowd. Snowden, with his 'Come to Jesus' style of revivalist oratory, was a powerful speaker and he caused great worry to the local Liberals. So much so, that shortly afterwards they organised a follow-up meeting addressed by Robson in an effort to head-off Labour's advance. His speech was an attempt to rebut socialism by showing how much his own political philosophy had in common with it. He argued that the nationalisation of land for town development was his preference and further that certain monopolies, 'especially gas, water, tramways and electricity, are better in municipal than in private hands, and the same principle may well be applied to mountains, moors and waste spaces'. (11) Doubtless the threat of Labour's advance forced Robson's hand, but in doing so, it stemmed the Party's progress at least until after Robson's day.

On the other hand, as late as 1908, the national Labour Party, which the LRC had become in 1906, wrote to the Trades Council inquiring why Labour was doing so poorly in South Shields. Clearly the Trades Council still found it difficult to break all its ties with the Liberals and its secretary conceded that discipline was proving difficult, resulting in competing working-class candidates. The difficulties in attaining a united approach to elections continued for a few more years. The early LRC proved to be somewhat of a failure as a consequence of continued Liberal domination in certain trade unions.

The Osborne Judgement of 1909 which threatened the ability of trade unions to participate in political action, concentrated the minds of their members on the question of political representation. The two elections in 1910 further stimulated this debate. Trade unionists in South Shields were not immune from these concerns and increasing interest developed in Labour representation. Towards the end of 1911, informal discussions were taking place between interested groups and on 10 January 1912 a conference was held in the town which decided to establish a South Shields Local Labour Party affiliated to the national Labour Party.

This was followed up on St Valentine's Day by the formal establishment of a permanent South Shields Labour Party. The initiative for this came from the ILP. The inaugural meeting took place at their headquarters, the Labour Hall in Chapter Row, and one of their members, Jimmy Curbison, took the chair whilst another activist, Charles Johnston, became secretary. Ten unions in all were represented on the executive in addition to Mrs Towns of the Women's Labour League. The most significant appointment however was that of A E Gompertz as assistant secretary. 'Gompy', as he became known, did more than any other individual in building up the local Labour Party. Although he resigned as assistant secretary due to a technicality at the March meeting, for the next half century, he served the movement as councillor, alderman, mayor, full-time secretary and agent - indeed to many in the town he was 'Mr Labour'.

The activists were intent on extending their influence by propaganda and organisation. Outdoor meetings were organised, principally in the Market Place, and in October

1912 a socialist propagandist, T Russell Williams, was engaged for a week's activity at a cost of £3 plus expenses. This was a new venture which stretched the financial resources of the organisation to the limit.

Great efforts were also expended in persuading further branches of trade unions to affiliate. This was not restricted only to unions and interestingly the League of the Blind affiliated as early as July 1912. Given the strength of the the mining union, deputations were sent to the three miners Lodges to join but initially they ran into difficulties. The Liberals on the lodge committees attempted to delay and deflect the approaches. Harton said no and the remaining two decided to ballot their members. Harton Lodge, however, quickly had a change of heart and on 2 July 1912 affiliated 1000 members and sent its three delegates. However, the Party had to wait two more years before Marsden and St Hilda Lodges formally affiliated, the latter then disaffiliating for a period before becoming permanently affiliated in 1920.

World War One brought about a political truce with the local Party deciding not to contest the municipal elections. The South Shields Party reflected the national divergence of opinion on the war with some members becoming conscientious objectors (COs) whilst the majority supported the war effort. In particular, Gompertz was a CO and suffered severely on account of this stance, spending three years in Armley Prison, Leeds, for his views. When the war ended and he returned to South Shields, he could only walk with the aid of crutches for several months due to the maltreatment he had received in prison. On the other hand the overwhelming majority decided that three of their number should serve on the local war recruiting-committee.

In spite of this divergence of attitudes on the war, the Party opposed Government plans for conscription, a view it re-affirmed consistently throughout the hostilities. Indeed, as time progressed their views hardened and they insisted on their opposition to the 'conscription of labour until there was conscription of capital'. Furthermore, members of differing views united together to 'express disgust' at the manner in which J Ramsay MacDonald was being personally abused on account of his pacifist stance.

Concerns of ordinary people on the home front were constantly being raised. The plight of soldiers' families was often highlighted and later in the war the position of discharged wounded soldiers caused consternation. In particular, the escalating price of food was a matter of constant complaint and of course the issue of housing, for so long a worry of the local activists, was raised repeatedly. As early as June 1914, the Party convened a day conference in South Shields on the housing problem and frequently castigated the local council for its failure to implement the Housing of the Working Classes Act.

In the second year of the war, the Party began to tire of the political truce and yearned again for political action. They began the process of selecting a parliamentary candidate and chose Joe Batey. His sponsoring union, the DMA, supplied a full-time agent, Jack Gilliland, who did much good organising work until the union withdrew support from Batey and transferred his agent to Chester-le-Street at the end of 1915. This change of policy by the DMA was because the Labour Party nationally felt they were 'claiming' too many constituencies. But it caused great disappointment in South Shields, for Batey was their 'favourite son'.

By the time of municipal elections in 1915, the local Party mustered 9 members of the Council;

Alderman J Cullen	(Marsden Miner)
Councillor J Dunlop	(Boilermakers Society)
Councillor C A Henderson	(NUR)
Councillor R Vine	(Harton Miner)
Councillor J Howe	(Harton Miner)
Councillor G Linney	(Marsden Miner)
Councillor J R Curbison	(ILP & Shop Assistants Union)
Councillor J Batey	(ILP & St Hilda Miner)
Councillor J Toll	(ILP & St Hilda Miner)

There was to be no change in the number of the Labour councillors for the duration of the war, all being returned to the council when their period of office expired. When the long-standing councillor, John Toll, died in 1917, he was replaced by a fellow miner, James Watson. Watson was, like Toll, a stalwart of St Hilda Lodge and later went on to be its president. He was appointed councillor under the war-time political truce. At the time of his appointment on 17 February 1917, St Hilda Lodge was not formally affiliated to the local Labour Party so technically Watson was not a member of the Labour Group. Toll had been, for in addition to being from St Hilda Lodge he was nominated by the ILP. Eventually, Watson joined the Group and gave many years of service to the Labour Party. This was the period when the Party locally and nationally was building up a reservoir of electoral support which was to see a great increase in Labour councillors in the following few years.

CHAPTER THREE

Building the Party: 1918-1945

The war did see the various Labour organisations trying to work together. By 9 June 1917, talks of an amalgamation between the two principal bodies, the Trades Council and the Labour Party, were so advanced that a schedule was agreed by the respective executives. However, the formal amalgamation awaited the national Labour Party's new constitution, and the South Shields Labour Party and Trades Council came into being on 21 February 1918. This arrangement was to last for over fifty years. There was one small hiccup in that the local Party still did not make provision for individual members - one had to be a member through an affiliated body. It was only following a complaint from the Labour Party headquarters in August 1918 that this was rectified.

Cllr G H Linney was elected chairman and Cllr J R Curbison, secretary. Most of the major unions were represented on the executive committee but not a single woman. However, the following month it was agreed to establish a women's section so the point had at least registered with the Party. It is worthy of note that whilst three miners' lodges, Boldon, Harton and Marsden, were affiliated, the oldest St Hilda's refused to do so until June 1920. Liberalism still had a strong hold with many miners.

Almost as soon as the reformed Party was established, moves were in hand again to choose a parliamentary candidate. On 9 March 1918, two potential candidates appeared for interview with the result that George Rowe, a boilermaker, defeated John Swan, a miner, by 55 votes to 22.

George Rowe was a councillor from across the River Tyne in North Shields. He had been elected to Tynemouth County Borough Council in 1913 and had a growing reputation in local government on Tyneside. But he was even more widely known in trade union circles. He had been born in 1872 in London's East End but had moved up to Willington Quay with his parents when he was ten. On leaving school he served his apprenticeship as a caulker at Palmer's Howdon yard. He joined the Boilermakers Society in 1891 and quickly showed an aptitude for trade union work. Soon he gained the confidence of his workmates becoming a full-time union official for the whole of Northumberland, Tyneside and North Durham. This involved representing the men in negotiations about wages and working conditions and thus he was well known to many thousands of men in shipyards and engineering works in South Shields. He had a strong personality, was a fluent and lucid orator and a formidable debater; clearly an appropriate choice for the town's Labour candidate.

About this time, rumours began to circulate that the sitting Liberal MP, C A Cochrane, who had been returned unopposed in a by-election in 1916 on Russell Rea's death, was about to retire. Furthermore, it was being said that the renegade trade union leader, J Havelock Wilson, was to contest the seat against the Labour Party.

In response, the local Party began a frenzied period of activity. Rowe's union, the boilermakers, contributed £200 towards the salary of an agent and the national party contributed £40. As a result, G McNamara, the deputy-secretary of the Weavers Association in Blackburn was appointed. One of the others considered but not appointed was Lillian Fenn, 'a lady organiser from headquarters'.

Mrs Fenn had gained quite a reputation and it was not too surprising that a woman was considered in South Shields. Although the initial local executive did not contain a woman this was out of character, for women had played an important part in the ILP in particular and a formal women's section was being formed.

Women occupied a significant role in the Labour Party throughout the North East of England and South Shields was no exception. In a region dominated by heavy industry, the men were active in their unions and it was often the women who in essence ran the local parties. The early party organisers realised the crucial role that women played and sought to develop that potential to the full. Initially under the guidance of the Northern Women's Organiser, from 1919-1929, Lilian Anderson Fenn and then for another 25 years under the indomitable Margaret Gibb, thousands upon thousands of women found their emancipation under Labour.

Unlike in certain other parts of the country, women in the North East of England traditionally did not do paid work outside the home. This was especially so in the mining areas where women were overloaded with the domestic work which was vital to ensure an almost continuous supply of hot water and food for their working families. But they often were able to attend meetings of Labour women's sections.

Furthermore, the women's organisations in the North East shrewdly managed to build upon the culture of collectivism in their neighbourhoods so that it was as natural for women in the industrial North East to join the women's sections of the Labour Party as in other districts it would have been to join the Women's Institute or Townswomen's Guild. In County Durham alone in the 1920s there were over 150 women's sections and a further 80 in Northumberland. Indeed, in South Shields there were 5 at one time; Central, East, South, West and Harton.

The South Shields women played their full part in the County Durham women's movement and always sent representatives to the regular weekend schools. To this day, they are never without representation at the annual Cober Hall Women's School. Another attraction they never missed was the annual women's Gala which was traditionally held at Wharton Park in Durham City. This Gala was based on the same principle as the Durham Miners' Gala, with the women's sections marching under their banners accompanied by brass bands; usually provided by the local colliery lodges. Held early in June, literally thousands attended this event and listened to many of the top speakers in the Labour movement. Invitations to speakers resulted from a ballot of the individual women's sections and it was a great honour to receive such an invitation.

Many women have followed in the footsteps of Cllr Mrs E Thorpe who won Tyne Dock in 1927 becoming not only Labour's first woman councillor but also the first woman on the council. Two years later she was followed by Cllr Mrs Mary Peel and then in 1932 by Cllr Mrs Margaret Sutton. Cllr Mrs Elizabeth Diamond who became an excellent Chair of Education in the 1970s and 1980s, and Cllr Mrs Lilian Jordison Chair of Leisure for most of the 1980s, were only two of the many women who held prominent positions on the council.

South Shields Women's Section at Durham Women's Gala, 1952
Left to right: Mrs Lawrenson, Mrs Croft, Cllr Mrs Roberts, Mrs Bertram, Mrs E Roberts
Cllr S Lloyd, Ald Mrs Glover, Chuter Ede, Mrs Leather, unknown, Ald Mrs Hart, Mrs Lucas

One of the women who would have worked to get Mrs Thorpe elected in Tyne Dock was Jane Byrne, Liz Diamond's mother. Mrs Byrne was one of the indefatigable women who worked incessantly for the Party yet never put herself forward for elected public office. They were indeed the backbone of the Party. But in addition to working for Labour she was married to a miner and brought up a family who themselves accepted her values of socialism and the duty to serve one's fellow citizens. She encouraged them to train for a profession. Liz became a teacher and was one of the most respected in the town. Her brother Henry went to medical school and worked in South Shields as a general practitioner before emigrating to Australia. It was an incredible family, with an outstanding mother and socialist. Jane Byrne was the archetypal woman upon whom the Labour Party in the North East of England was founded.

The women's section, still alive and kicking in 1992, has served the Party well throughout its existence. It has many members and meets regularly, playing an active role in both the political and the social life of the local Party. Furthermore, its members are always active in regional meetings and events.

Meanwhile, the Party had found new office premises in Edinburgh Buildings at 34 King Street but then were immediately thrown into a real quandary. The rumours of a pending by-election were proved to be true in the late summer of 1918.

During the course of the war, the rumoured candidate, Havelock Wilson, had been active in forming the Merchant Seamen's League (MSL), and as the leading light in this organisation he addressed meetings throughout Britain including the North East. He always expressed strident anti-German sentiments which pandered to the jingoist element in the population and nowhere more so than in a place such as South Shields where many seamen had lost their lives as their ships were sunk in the hostilities.

By August, Wilson was out and about in South Shields. He gained publicity by donating £50 to the mayor's Tyne Distressed Seamen's Fund and the following week announced his intention to fight the next election in the town. By the end of the month, he had obtained the endorsement of the local Liberals who unanimously agreed that, 'Mr Havelock Wilson be selected as the prospective Liberal and Labour candidate' for South Shields. Early in September, Wilson rejected the Lib-Lab designation and told the TUC in Derby that he would stand as a 'patriotic trade union candidate'.

The election speculation mounted and the Tories discussed endorsing Wilson who announced the MSL would donate £2000 to the Town's 'Fun Week'. On 13 October he called a mass meeting of trade unionists only, chaired by George Birkett of the Iron Founders Society, and was duly adopted as 'patriotic trade union candidate'. This was a clever move by Wilson as trade union membership cards were a prerequisite for entry into the meeting, but even then he failed to gain official trade union endorsement. But Wilson knew what he was doing. He was trying to undermine Rowe's base support by portraying himself as the true representative of the workingman.

Havelock Wilson was an experienced and skilful politician and on the face of it an ideal candidate for South Shields. He was president of the National Sailors and Firemens Union with many members in the town. He had been born in nearby Sunderland and had been elected as a Labour MP for Middlesbrough in 1892. No sooner had he been elected than he commenced building bridges with the Liberals who supported him from 1895 to 1910. In effect he had reverted to being a Lib/Lab MP, campaigning against ILP and LRC candidates.

He was a trade union leader of the most ruthless kind. Manny Shinwell recounts that when he was trying to establish an alternative trade union for seamen, Wilson took out a contract on him to be murdered with the result that when Shinwell was addressing a public meeting in Glasgow, the wrong man was taken out and shot dead standing right next to him!

Shinwell knew South Shields well, having lived there on two separate occasions. He always maintained he did not like the town in view of his unhappy experiences there. In his autobiography, *Lead with the Left*, he devoted some space to South Shields. His first visit was in 1892 when his father, leaving his family in London, established a seamen's outfitters shop and the eight-year old Emmanuel made the long journey by rail from London on his own to join him. He describes his living conditions thus:

'His business premises consisted of a front-shop and one room behind, where we ate, cooked and slept. Sometimes I would be left in charge - between the ages of eight and nine! - while he went aboard vessels in search of customers. My recollection is that the main source of income came from the sale of mattresses to sailors who, in those days on tramp vessels, had to provide their own bedding. He bought several yards of canvas, sewed them up, filled them with straw and sold them for as much as he could get, usually a shilling or fractionally over.' (1)

Eventually the business failed and the Shinwells moved north to Glasgow.

About the turn of the century, Shinwell's father's business in Glasgow was failing and the family moved to South Shields again. Manny went with them. He was on the point of enlisting in a boxing booth circuit when the call of love dissuaded him. Before leaving Glasgow he 'had become friendly with a young lady' who suggested he should return to Scotland. He could only resolve the problem of the money for the fare by selling his collection of books to a stall-holder on South Shields market - a painful experience. He wrote:

> 'for the second time I departed from Shields. I hoped I had finished with the place, but some years later when I was national organiser of the Marine Workers Union, Shields was one of the ports included in my itinerary.' (2)

Many years later, Shinwell returned to address an evening meeting. He was booked into bed and breakfast accommodation with a Party supporter near the Chichester area of the town. Later when he met the organiser of the visit he was most disgruntled with the accommodation for without regard for his Jewish background they gave him 'bacon and egg' for breakfast! Shinwell and South Shields were plainly incompatible.

Shinwell's experience of Wilson was not unique, for Wilson associated with bad company. One of his main colleagues was the notorious Horatio Bottomley, publisher of *John Bull*. Bottomley was an MP with a shady career which culminated in his expulsion from the House of Commons in 1922 having been found guilty of fraud and sentenced to seven years in prison.. But before then, he travelled up to Shields to speak for Wilson. Yet another companion was the former socialist MP, Victor Grayson, whose flat Wilson visited frequently.

Grayson had been elected sensationally at a by-election in Colne Valley in 1907 and had become the darling of the left-wing of the Labour Party for a short time. He enlisted in the New Zealand forces during World War One and was wounded at Passchendaele, the same battle at which the local activist Cuth Barrass was. He then travelled the country with Wilson, accompanied by a tank, Nelson, raising money for the war effort. The tank was in South Shields on 31 January 1918. Grayson had connections with espionage work and was to disappear mysteriously in September 1920. By the time Wilson was candidate for South Shields he too was undoubtedly a fellow member of the embryonic secret service.

In mid-October 1918 Cochrane duly resigned. The Conservatives decided to join the Liberals and support Wilson. This forced the local Labour Party into a corner. They had a candidate in George Rowe, but were short of financial resources. By law, there had to be a general election in a matter of months. The national Labour Party had advised them not to contest the by-election when a deputation from the local Party met Arthur Henderson MP in Newcastle in September. With this in mind, they decided to save the boilermakers' money. However, by doing so they allowed Wilson a free run and an unopposed return with the result that he assumed the status and prestige of being the town's MP.

Meanwhile, the local Party strategists were conscious of the need to attract the sizeable Irish and Catholic vote in the town. They were aware of how the Irish vote in neighbouring Jarrow had affected Parliamentary elections and were determined to learn from the experience. Encouragement had already been given through the Irish Labour Party with its branches in the town, centrally and at Tyne Dock, both of which played a full part in the activities of the local Party. However, in an attempt to reinforce the relationship, it was decided to invite Charles Diamond, the editor of *Catholic News*, to address a meeting at the Palace Theatre in Frederick Street on 3 November 1918. It is clear from the Party's minute-books that this was adjudged a particularly important function.

Rowe himself was in the pro-war faction of the Labour Party. He had an exemplary war record which was widely appreciated by the authorities during the war. He was appointed a member of the Armaments Committee of the North East Coast, invited to join the Munitions Board and then in 1917 was made a member of the prestigious Committee of Protection, in connection with which he travelled all over the United Kingdom. Indeed it is hard to imagine anyone with a more exemplary war record on the home front and this was recognised officially following the hostilities when he was awarded the Order of the British Empire 'for war-time services'. But even he had no answer to Wilson's blatant jingoistic approach. In the few weeks between his unopposed return as MP and the next election, Wilson played this card repeatedly. By the end of November 1918, both the Liberals and the Conservatives had endorsed Wilson again. Meanwhile, on the 21st of the same month, George Rowe formally launched his own election campaign with a public meeting in the Palace Theatre supported by Alderman Dunlop and Councillor C A Henderson of the Railwaymen's Union.

The choice of these two personalities reflected the acumen of Rowe. They were both well-know trade-union personalities in the town and had strong followings in different sections of the electorate. Dunlop was a senior member of the council and employed as a boilermaker at

George Rowe, Labour Candidate, South Shields, 1918.

Readhead's shipyard. An outspoken advocate of socialism, he had been born in Renfrew, Scotland in 1865 and worked in many shipbuilding communities in the North of England.

Councillor Charlie Henderson was a much quieter but no less fervent supporter of the socialist and trade-union cause - he even had his son christened in 1896, Hardie Mann Blatchford, such was his faith in the new philosophy and its leaders. A railwayman to his fingertips, he joined the ILP in 1905 and represented the community of Simonside on the council and was one of the most respected personalities in the town. He was a year younger than Dunlop and had developed into a formidable organiser. He joined the Amalgamated Society of Railway Servants in 1890 and three years later was elected secretary of the Tyne Dock No 1 Branch. In those days thousands of railwaymen worked in the town, mainly in connection with the traffic of coal to the docks. In no time he had built-up his branch membership from 270 to 1600. Later he went on to represent the North East on the executive of the National Union of Railwaymen, which the ASRS became. The union's General Secretary, J H Thomas, was a long-time personal friend and confidant. The Labour leader Keir Hardie was another good friend of Henderson. Like George Rowe, Henderson was supportive of the war effort and was a member of the Military Tribunal. In recognition of his efforts he was made a Member of the British Empire and later, in 1922, appointed a JP. His son, preferring his name-sake Blatchford's view of the war to that of the pacifist Keir Hardie, joined up and fought in France. Within the family folklore, it is reputed of his enlistment that it was the final straw leading to Hardie's death often said to be as a result of a broken heart over the war.

Given the circumstances, the choice of the two men as principal sponsors was a wise and astute move by Rowe and the local Labour Party.

When the election was declared, the Labour Party fought a vigorous campaign but there was much for them to learn in this their first parliamentary contest. Wilson now stood as a 'Trade Union Coalitionist Candidate' thus challenging the very base of Rowe's working-class support. The mood in the town was very anti-German and Wilson played to this unhesitatingly. In addition, this was the 'coupon election' when certain candidates were given the patriotic endorsement and Wilson was again one of the beneficiaries.

Furthermore, this was also a khaki election and some of the Labour leaders such as Ramsay MacDonald and Philip Snowden had been anti-war. This harmed the Labour Party nationally and was aggravated locally by the fact that early local activists such as Gompertz and R H Noble were also prominent conscientious objectors.

All in all, this was not the most propitious election for the local Party to cut its Parliamentary teeth on and the result was hardly surprising.

<u>South Shields General Election 1918</u>

J Havelock Wilson (TU-Coal)	19,514
George Rowe (Lab)	6,425
majority	<u>13,089</u>

The local activists quickly shook off the defeat and set about the task of improving their electoral base. A women's section was formally established but the financial position was such that after much debate and heart-searching, the Party had to dispense with their full-time agent.

The electorate in the town was now 50,584 compared with only 18,320 at the time of the previous general election in 1910. Part of this increase was due to women aged over 30 being given the vote for the first time but another reason was the number of men being enfranchised. It has not been widely understood that while on paper all adult men had the vote since 1884, in practice the registration laws prohibited many of them from voting. In order to register to vote, certain rights of property had to be established and for many single men this often proved impossible.

In South Shields, as late as 1911, the position was:

Adult Male Pop.	Electorate	Voteless Men
26,065	18,709	7,356 (28.8%)

Therefore, almost one man in three was without the vote and the position for unmarried men was even worse. (3) In 1911, it was estimated that 76% of single men were ineligible to vote. The general level of disenfranchisement created a difficulty for the new party. A large number of the younger men, many of whom favoured the ideas of Labour, were prohibited from voting, thus weakening the position of the party electorally. The continuing progress towards all adults actually possessing the vote was a growing benefit to the Labour Party in South Shields as elsewhere.

With the end of the war and the return of men from the trenches, housing became a major political issue. South Shields had long had a major housing problem. There was chronic overcrowding and slum conditions were rife in certain parts of the town, especially in the wards near the river, with the accompanying health problems and high death rates.

As early as 1891, the town's Medical Officer of Health, Dr Eustace Hill, drew attention to this poor housing when he referred to parts of Holborn in his annual report: 'All such property should undoubtedly be closed as unfit for habitation....it must be thoroughly understood that this type of property should not be allowed to exist a day longer than is necessary...So long as that class of property is allowed to exist, sickness and death must be in excess amongst its inhabitants.'

Nothing happened, however, for almost three decades. By 1907 only Gateshead, of all the boroughs in England, had worse overcrowding. In that year, the council refused to act upon the recommendation of its medical officer to replace the filthy privy receptacle system of sanitation with a water-carriage one. It was against this background that the Labour councillors tried to make housing one of their main electoral planks. But with only 9 councillors out of 45 by 1914, they could effect no real progress.

World War One raised the issue to a new level and consequently the Labour Party stepped up its campaign. Its members were instrumental in forming tenant defence leagues. As the war progressed, the need for improving the housing situation in the town became more urgent. In 1918, an official survey estimated that out of a total population in the town of 105,000, no less than 35,000 lived in severely overcrowded conditions. The population density was nearly 48 persons per acre compared with the average of 21 in other English county boroughs. Little wonder that the death rate was so much higher than in other comparable towns.

Clearly something had to be done if the slogan of soldiers returning to a 'land fit for heroes' was to be matched. In December 1917 the mayor, Andrew Anderson, an Independent councillor and local businessman, chaired a newly-established committee of Housing and Town Planning. The long-serving Labour councillor, Jimmy Dunlop, was made vice-chairman.

The Labour councillors kept up the pressure for the local authority to take advantage of new legislation to provide new houses for working people. In March 1918, the council decided to enter negotiations to purchase 196 acres of the Cleadon Park Estate at a cost of £54 per acre. (4) This was mainly farm land and was just outside the then borough boundaries.

The saga of this purchase is amazing. The mayor had been trying to buy this land privately for himself but told the council that his offer had been turned down and therefore he could freely act for the council. He travelled to London to negotiate on its behalf with the seller, Kirkley Trustees. On his return the mayor explained that as the local authority obviously needed some time to reach decisions and as the sale had to be completed speedily he had purchased the Estate himself but would re-sell it at the price he had paid for it. A month later he requested that he retain the mansion and ten acres of gardens which the council had been intending to use as a TB sanatorium. By June rumours were circulating that something was amiss and a public inquiry was launched. By October the mayor was backtracking on his offer. The Town Clerk then discovered that the mayor had lied to the council about his intentions and actions. In November he resigned from the mayoralty and council and eventually the council bought the land as the original sale fell through.

It was two further years before it transpired that the mayor had been working in collusion with the Smith's Dock Company to buy the land in order for them to build houses for their own workers. This had the backing of some unions for their members were to be allowed to buy their homes. This raised an interesting point as to whether the council should provide houses for purchase or for rent. Some of the unions preferred the former and even the St Hilda miners were trying to instigate a scheme for their members to buy subsidised houses which Harton Coal Company would build.

By 1921, 600 houses had been built. The problem came to a head when it was realised that the rents for the Cleadon Park houses would be too high for most working people and would in fact do little to resolve the slum housing problem.

In the years immediately following the war, the number of Labour councillors gaining election more than doubled. By December 1923, the Housing Committee, now under the chairmanship of Alderman Dunlop, proposed the selling of 290 houses then under construction and this was seconded by another Labour stalwart, Cllr Curbison. A row broke out, with four Labour councillors, R H Noble (Shields Ward), John Cheeseman, George Linney (both of Tyne Dock) and Will Pearson (Laygate) opposing the move. They argued it was wrong to sell the houses when there was a drastic need for rented accommodation. Cllr Edmondson of St Hilda Miner's Lodge argued for sale on the basis that people had the right to own their homes. Seventeen Labour councillors opposed the rebels and voted for the sale of the houses.

In 1926, following the General Strike, another group of houses came up for sale and in light of the massive unemployment in the town, the Labour Party as a whole opposed the sale. Of the 1923 sale nearly half the purchasers had not been on the council's waiting list. Insecurity of employment was another restraint and even Alderman Dunlop opposed this phase of sales.

Almost 1000 council houses had been built since 1919, but the slums remained. The Cleadon Park estate, whether for rent or purchase, only benefited the better off members of the working class. However, what was interesting was the divergence of opinion in the Labour ranks, with former extreme left-wing activists such as Curbison and Dunlop joining with certain trade unionists to argue for working-people to buy their own homes whilst many of the more moderate councillors joined those representing the wards with the worst housing problems and argued solely for rented houses.

In addition to housing, the issue which dominated the Party's debates and actions throughout the twenties and thirties, was unemployment. The North East of England as a whole suffered grievously from the lack of work once the war ended and South Shields suffered even worse than the regional average. By 1934, the number seeking work in the town had risen to 30.9%. Repeatedly, the Party discussed and campaigned on the issue. Resolutions were passed and despatched to all levels of authority. In the early 1920s, they permitted the local Unemployment Committee to affiliate to the Party without payment. They even held back from running a candidate in a winnable council seat and encouraged one of their own activists, Tom Mulgrew, to stand as an official Unemployment Committee candidate, although as it happened to no avail. The Labour members of the Board of Guardians consistently fought for more generous payments to those who found themselves in financial difficulties. The curse of unemployment was regarded universally in the Party as one of the worst evils of the capitalist system. A century after the formation of the Party, unemployment in the town remains obstinately and unacceptably high; being the highest of any travel-to-work area in England. In April 1992, 18.3% of the workforce in South Shields were unemployed and 25.6% of men. Party activists still regard unemployment as one of the greatest problems of the town.

Meanwhile, within the Party, in May 1919, only six months following the election, they had decided to begin the procedure of selecting a new parliamentary candidate, but progress was slow. Two months later they also decided to regularise their role in local government and established a formal Labour Group on the Borough Council.

The position of Labour councillors was still proving difficult and somewhat confusing. There were, in essence, 'official' and 'unofficial' Labour candidates. The official ones were those nominated by one of the affiliated bodies and approved by the South Shields Labour Party. These were people such as Charles Henderson, nominated by the NUR or Charles Smith by the Boilermakers Society. In addition, there were other bodies affiliated such as the ILP or the local Irish Labour Party which had two branches. Cllr Curbison was nominated by the ILP and W McAnany by the Irish Labour Party. The unofficial 'Labour' councillors were those such as Cllrs Edmondson and Watson, both St Hilda miners, whose Lodge was not affiliated to the Party. Following the affiliation of the Lodge in July 1920, they were admitted into the Group. Likewise Cllr Amos Ayres, was a longstanding councillor, nominated by his society, the river pilots, and in September 1920, the Labour Party decided not to oppose him and he in turn agreed to join the formal Group.

A slightly more complicated case was that of the Cooperative Movement. They ran candidates and a deputation met the Labour Party officials in 1920 with the view of reaching some accommodation. The local Cooperative officials were individual members of the Labour Party but they explained they could not formally join the Group until a decision was taken nationally on the precise role of the Cooperative Party. An accommodation was actually reached, the Coop candidate was unopposed by Labour and it was minuted shortly afterwards that Labour election posters would be displayed in certain Coop shops. This agreement was facilitated by the good relationship between the Labour Party and the Cooperative Societies, with Cllr Joe Batey being president of the South Shields Cooperative Society for many years and Cllr Charles Henderson also being closely involved with the Tyne Dock Society.

As the years progressed, the relationship between the Party and the cooperative movement in the town grew even closer. For almost forty years, 'the co-op' and Labour became synonymous in the eyes of many. The majority of Labour people tended to shop at 'the store', and dividend numbers are remembered to this day. The system of dividend payments based on the amount you had spent was an important part of many working-class budgets in the years before World War Two and for several years afterwards. Gradually, the 'divi' went, and faced with competition from the supermarket chains, the retail dominance of the cooperative societies began to decline until now there is only one shop remaining in the whole South Shields constituency. Nevertheless, the South Shields and the Tyne Dock Cooperative Societies and the Boldon one, with a shop in Boldon Lane until the 1980s, played an important role in the Party's history. To this day, there are four delegates to the general committee from the Cooperative Party and the Cooperative Women's

Guild still regularly pays its affiliation fees as it has for decades. The philosophy of cooperation fits easily and comfortably into that of Labour in South Shields as elsewhere.

Following the November 1919 local elections, however, the official Labour group comprised:

Chairman	Cllr G H Linney
Secretary	Cllr J R Curbison
Aldermen	J Dunlop and C Henderson
Councillors	Bradley, Chapman, Howe, Rowley, Smith, Stewart, Surtees and Vine.

As more and more trade union branches became affiliated the problem between the different 'Labour' candidates became minimised. By 1927 the composition of the town council was; 22 Labour, 18 Liberals, 20 Anti-Socialists. Thus the various groups supporting Labour representation were finally beginning to coalesce after more than 30 years of division and tension.

In the summer of 1920, moves were again afoot to select a parliamentary candidate and the Party formally invited 'the DMA to make South Shields one of their constituencies'. South Shields was estimated to have 15% of its electorate working as miners employed mainly at Harton, Marsden and St Hilda collieries.

Various personalities were actively considered as potential candidates including Charles Trevelyan of Wallington Hall in Northumberland. He had been Liberal MP for Spen Valley in Yorkshire and was later to become the Labour MP for Newcastle Central and President of the Board of Education in the first two Labour Governments. Another fancied candidate was Jos Ritson, a checkweighman from Monkwearmouth Colliery and a Sunderland councillor. He was later MP for Durham City and great uncle of Joyce Quin, herself one time MEP for the district including South Shields and then following the 1987 General Election, MP for Gateshead East.

There was an interesting development in proceedings in December when the local Party rejected a move by the Communist Party to be affiliated. The executive committee meanwhile had been sifting out potential candidates and settled on Will Lawther. He served on the executive of the DMA and was secretary of the Victoria Garesfield Lodge near Chopwell in West Durham.

On 14 January 1922, twenty-three affiliated bodies were represented at the Parliamentary selection conference with Will Lawther as the only nominee. He was duly selected and was endorsed by his union, the DMA, who also bore the brunt of the financial implications of his selection. The union also provided an agent which in due course caused a minor difficulty over precisely to whom the candidate was responsible and the General Management Committee debated the issue as 'who has control of the candidate; the DMA or the Party?'. The divisions and suspicions were clearly still lurking under the surface.

Ten months later, when the General Election was announced, the Labour Party felt it necessary to issue a statement that Will Lawther 'was not a communist'. This was deemed essential for Will had something of a left-wing image coming as he did from a family of politically active miners in Chopwell, which was known throughout the region as 'Little Moscow'. In South Shields, with only a minority of the electorate being miners and with a sizeable middle-class vote, it was obviously felt important to disassociate the candidate from the communists.

The local campaign was vigorous and exciting. The patriotic mania, so dominant in 1918, had abated and some of the activists scented victory. Huge numbers were drawn to their public meetings which culminated in thousands attending an eve-of-poll meeting at the Mill Dam. It was estimated that 10,000 people were present with colour being added by the banners and bands from four collieries; Boldon, Harton, Marsden and St Hilda. Bill Blyton, later Lord Blyton, who was present at that meeting claimed it was in fact a pyrrhic victory and cost Labour the seat. He maintained that the very size and enthusiasm of the meeting gave notice to their opponents that Labour could actually win and this led to a consolidation of the Liberal vote to stop the dreaded Labour Party. Immediately following the meeting, the Conservatives, who were backing Wilson, sent the message out to their supporters, urging them to switch their votes to the Liberal.

As was usual, Bill's judgement was almost certainly correct for when the vote was counted on 15 November it was initially too close to call. It took eight and a half hours to complete the count with numerous recounts and at one stage only two votes separated the two leading candidates. The sitting MP, now running under the National Liberal banner with Conservative support, was at the bottom of the poll.

South Shields General Election 1922

E A Harney (Lib)	15,760
Will Lawther (Lab)	15,735
J Havelock Wilson (Nat Lib)	8,121
majority	25

The local Party activists were disappointed with the result but not dismayed. They immediately asked the DMA to allow Lawther to be the candidate again for it was clear that another election could not be far off. They agreed and appointed a half-time agent. Political propaganda efforts were stepped-up with the Labour leader, J Ramsay MacDonald speaking in the town on 29 July 1923 at the Queens Theatre. Other meetings were held addressed by Sydney Webb MP, Mardy Jones MP, George Lansbury MP, Jack Lawson MP and Manny Shinwell MP.

However, in spite of two further active Parliamentary campaigns at the elections of 1923 and 1924, Lawther was never able to come close again. The opportunity had been lost in 1922 when there had been a chance of a split Liberal vote. When the anti-socialist forces realised that this could lead to a Labour victory they closed ranks. These elections were straight fights between the two parties with the Tory voters backing the Liberals with the following results.

South Shields General Elections	1923	1924
E A Harney (Lib)	22,912	23,171
Will Lawther (Lab)	15,717	16,852
majority	7,195	6,319

J Ramsay MacDonald entering Queens Theatre,
South Shields, 29 July 1923. MacDonald (left),
Cuth Barrass (third from right), Will Lawther (second from right).

Bill Blyton who, as a young miner, was active in both campaigns argued that following the 1924 defeat, the South Shields Party realised that they could not win the seat with a miner as candidate. It was felt that whilst a miner could draw the homogeneous mining vote, he nevertheless failed to attract the same degree of loyalty from other trade unionists who indeed were often suspicious of the mining solidarity. In particular, there was some tension and rivalry between the miners and the shipyard workers. This sentiment was shared by another veteran, Margaret Sutton, who recalled that Chuter Ede was 'the right candidate for Shields because he was dead centre...he got Liberal votes that Will Lawther would not have got'.

Nevertheless, Will Lawther was a good candidate and he succeeded in raising the profile of the Party, increasing his share of the vote each time he fought the seat. He really established the Labour Party in South Shields as a political force to be reckoned with at the parliamentary level.

Will had been born at Choppington, Northumberland in 1889 and moved to County Durham where he had been active in the miners union from an early age. Following his candidature in South Shields he moved onto Barnard Castle where he was MP from 1929-31. He then turned his attention primarily to trade unionism being a member of the TUC General Council from 1935-54 and president of the Miners Federation of Great Britain, later the NUM, from 1939-54. Eventually, the miner from 'Little Moscow' also became a Knight of the Realm.

This was a far cry from his early days when he was regarded as somewhat of a firebrand and was on the Party's extreme left wing. He actively supported the suffragettes and when Connie Lewcock, a well-known Newcastle suffragette and Labour activist, planned to blow-up Durham Cathedral, it was Will who had supplied the explosives to her. Thankfully she decided at the last minute to abort her plans because she could not devise a way of escaping from her target alive and so the world's number one building was saved for posterity.

Meanwhile the Party went about strengthening its organisation. By the end of 1924, two women's sections were established and operating fully and a further two were in the pipeline.

The 1920s was the decade when the Labour Party really established itself in South Shields concluding in its standard bearer becoming the MP. Following the disappointment of the 1918 election defeat, the Government's inability to deal with the social problems became obvious to all, and disillusionment with the two established political parties of the day grew. The three General Elections of 1922, 1923 and 1924, although not successful for Labour, forced the local Party to develop its activities. Electoral activity at municipal level intensified with resulting success. Party activities developed and many new recruits were made to the Party and to socialism - when 'to be a socialist was to be known as a bolshevik' as Charles Smith and other pioneers recalled.

When the Party found itself without a headquarters in August 1920, the Marsden Miners lent it their hall in Imeary Street (later St Bede's Parochial Hall). Meetings were held there in addition to the open-air meetings on Sunday summer evenings at the Market Place where the Party had a recognised slot following the Salvation Army at 7 pm. Indeed, so successful were these outdoor meetings that in the early 1920s they alternated their venue between the Market Place and the Fountain, Slake

Terrace in Tyne Dock. At one stage yet another venue was
the Wouldhave Memorial near the seafront.

Bill Blyton felt that these were the critical years
when the Party locally really made the political
breakthrough and established itself, although a few years
had yet to elapse before the Party's strength was fully
realised in the ballot-box and the Liberal dominance
finally swept aside.

The tradition of an annual May Day event became
established during this period. The first was in 1919 and
this was sufficiently successful for the Party to repeat it
the following year. In 1920, they decided upon an outdoor
rally in Bents Park, prior to which they marched along a
route of Westoe Parade, Laygate Lane, Green Street, the
Market Place, King Street and Ocean Road to the
accompaniment of the Marsden Colliery Band. The
following year, they decided upon an indoor meeting at
the Marsden Miners' Hall which was preceded by a similar
march but this time even grander, for the four colliery
bands accompanied by their banners participated. It
must have proved a grand spectacle, prior to a mass
meeting addressed by Will Lawther, a firebrand of an
orator, and prominent local councillors.

At a more mundane and routine level, Margaret
Sutton vividly recalls canvassing in the 1920s and early
1930s. She contested the Hadrian Ward for four
consecutive years from 1929 and this experience
persuaded her of the desperate need to improve housing
in the town. She recounted her experiences near the river-
front, where big houses built originally for the
shipowners, were split-up and let-off in rooms.
Sometimes up to fourteen shared the same backyard and
this made for easy canvassing. A soap-box was found and
an impromptu public meeting followed, and in her own

May Day March, Women's Section and St Hilda Lodge, c 1920.

words 'you then got them all looking out of windows and listening to you...it was something new. There was no TV, no wireless, so anyone talking and they were there. You got your canvassing done champion then.'

Many of the earliest pioneers were still active and beginning to see their early dreams come to fruition. Some, such as Jimmy Dunlop and Jimmy Curbison, had formally joined the local establishment in that they had both become mayors of the town - but they remained far from establishment in spirit. Others had become councillors; a Scot, Bob Morgan, George Linney, the Marsden miners' official, Jack Thompson and Tom Mulgrew. Yet others worked tirelessly for the movement with no civic recognition, such as Teddy Towns, who had been active from almost the beginning and who never gave up his struggle on behalf of the movement. He was a charming-man, the salt of the earth who worked ceaselessly for the Labour Party.

There were the colourful characters as well, such as Bill Cooper and the Reverend Basil Viney, a Unitarian minister. Bill Cooper had trained for the priesthood but had given it up before ordination. He was over seventy and by the 1920s was blind. Bill Blyton recalls walking down Fowler Street during the 1921 miners strike with Bill Cooper when he espied the Reverend Viney approaching them pushing a hand-cart piled high with vegetables and fruit for the church harvest festival. As they stopped for a chat, the blind-man ran his hands over the produce and suggested to the minister a hymn to be sung the following day:

'We plough the fields and scatter
the good seed on the land.
But we don't get the harvest
I'd have you understand.
We plough the fields in sunshine
We plough the fields in rain
But we don't get the potatoes,
The turnips nor the grain.
And all good things around us,
are sent from heaven above
and the landlord comes from God knows where
which proves that God is love'

Perhaps predictably, even the socialist minister could not have that 'hymn' sung at his harvest festival in spite of the fact that the Agricultural Workers' Union was one of the stalwart affiliates of the South Shields Labour Party: another indication of how the town has changed over the century.

Religion and ethical socialism were blurred and yet intertwined. As an example of this, the early Labour pioneers in South Shields held a socialist Sunday school for children in the St Hilda's Miners' Hall in Maxwell Street.

Bill Blyton again recounts one occasion when he eavesdropped on Bill Cooper who was taking the Sunday school and was explaining to the children the ethics of capitalist society. Having done this, he finished his talk by reciting a little rhyme which in his opinion illustrated the capitalist system.

'Twinkle, twinkle little star
up in the sky so blue.
Its a good job you're up so high
or the boss would pinch you too.'

By parodying well known hymns, rhymes and sayings, the early socialists were able to catch the imagination of young people. This approach, coupled with the impoverished physical surroundings in which they lived, meant that towns such as South Shields proved receptive breeding grounds for the Labour philosophy.

The Party in South Shields, however, did not fully develop the all-embracing socialist sub-culture which emerged in parts of Lancashire and Yorkshire. There, members based their activities on clubs with permanent premises which in effect became oases where they could spend their spare time in an environment dominated by socialist ethics and ideas. These venues became centres for a wide variety of social as well as political happenings. They acted as reading rooms,centres for sewing classes and choirs, in addition to being rendezvous for clarion-type cycling or rambling clubs. Only later did they supply alcoholic beverages. At spasmodic periods throughout the 1920s the local Party did attempt to venture into these activities with some limited success. Apparently, Jimmy Curbison, who managed the local cooperative society's boot and shoe repair shop, and Dick Noble, who ran a small joiner's shop, both sited at the top of Victoria Road, did plan such a club. This did come to fruition albeit in a different form than was originally envisaged. The Labour and Social Club, many of whose members are keen Party supporters, reputedly came from this initiative. But it was not really the same type of Labour or socialist club as had been established in West Yorkshire, some of which survive in the 1990s. That the Party in South Shields had such difficulty in obtaining their own premises in the early years probably precluded this development and, furthermore, village or village-type communities seemed to lend themselves more easily to this approach than was the case in the large towns.

The industrial disputes of the decade, especially the miners strike of 1921 and the General Strike of 1926, served to reinforce the Party's message for the election of working-people. Chuter Ede gave great assistance to the miners during the latter strike and helped strengthen further the bond between the Labour Party and the miners. A bond which, over the years, was to grow from strength to strength. The strikes did clearly raise the political awareness of working-people generally in the town.

Such was the progress that in 1927, the local Party secretary, Alec Stephenson, could report that the year had seen an 'advance in the face of accumulated difficulties due to the severe industrial struggles of 1926'. There was an increase in male membership but a slight decrease amongst the women which was 'due to the inability of many of the women to attend actively, owing to the added work in the home through the operation of the Eight Hour Day in the mines'.

In December 1926 it was decided to establish a 'young people's section'. Moves were also made to set up a Labour Party brass band and a choir. This was not an uncommon phenomenon for the Party was coming to be seen as more than just a political body. The Labour Group had become a well established force on the Borough Council but had yet to attain control. As early as 1908, Jack Cullen had been appointed an alderman, to be followed by Dunlop and Henderson and in November 1925 Cllr Curbison became the first Labour mayor of the town. Labour had become an accepted part of the local political scene.

Although encouraged by these successes, the Constituency Party still had eyes on capturing the parliamentary seat. The net was cast wider than previously and the chief women's officer of the national Party, Dr Marion Phillips, was actively being promoted. She was not successful in South Shields but went on to be one of the two Labour MPs for Sunderland in 1929.

By April 1926, the various nominees had been narrowed down to two and a selection conference was held on 2 May. One of these two was Colonel Arthur Lynch who managed to get himself detained in Athens and was thus unable to attend the selection conference, although he did promise £100 per year towards the cost of an agent. His absence did not help him.

The successful candidate, by 47 votes to 28, was a man who was to serve the people of South Shields well for almost 40 years, Alderman J Chuter Ede. Chuter Ede had briefly been MP for Mitcham in Surrey following a by-election victory in 1923 and was sponsored by the National Union of Teachers who provided £250 per annum towards an agent's expenses. He was actively supported by a prominent local Labour activist, Cuthbert Barrass, later to be a councillor when he retired from teaching in 1945.

Cuth Barrass had been determined to bring Chuter Ede to South Shields. He himself was a well-known teacher in the town and was highly respected amongst the ordinary Party members. As early as 1906 he was speaking throughout the North East of England on educational matters from Labour platforms. In the year leading up to Pete Curran's by-election success in neighbouring Jarrow in 1907, he was a prominent platform supporter and thereafter he was much in demand at ILP meetings. During World War One he served as a stretcher-bearer with the Green Howards and was awarded the Military Medal for conspicuous bravery. He was wounded at the Battle of Passchendaele and spent eight months as a prisoner-of-war. His influence was enhanced in 1925 when he was appointed a magistrate for South Shields. Cuth Barrass remained as one of Chuter Ede's principal local confidants and friends. The MP owed a great deal over the years to the head-teacher.

At just that moment, the General Strike was declared and with four pits in its immediate vicinity, South Shields was badly affected. One person who came to the fore during this period was Bill Blyton of Harton Colliery, later to be Lord Blyton of South Shields. When Bill was elected in 1945 as Labour MP for the adjoining seat of Houghton-le-Spring, characteristically the first action he took was to repay the loan he had incurred during the General Strike.

In 1927 there was a dispute with the police over public meetings in the market place and at the end of 1928, Bill Blyton was again in the news when a writ was issued against him for a speech made at the market place. Following an apology by the young miner, the matter was dropped before it reached the court.

Gradually the miners were worn down and forced back to work. The bitterness remained and no doubt was of assistance to Chuter Ede when the election was called in 1929. The Party had been strengthening its organisation and propaganda role. Prominent MPs such as George Lansbury, a future Labour leader, as well as other national party leaders continued to visit the town. In 1928 Ernie Gompertz was selected as Chuter Ede's agent, a role he was to fulfil for eight successive elections.

The election of 1929 proved to be extremely eventful and exciting. The Liberal candidate, Harney, died within days of the nomination period and after a hectic

J Chuter Ede's Victory, May 1929.

campaign, Chuter Ede scraped in by a mere 40 votes. The figures were:

South Shields General Election 1929

James Chuter Ede (Lab)	18,938
H B Robson (Lib)	18,898
W Nunn (Con)	7,110
majority	40

When the result was declared, Chuter Ede was borne into a crowd of supporters on the shoulders of two stalwarts, Councillors McAnany and Thompson. Bedecked in their green and white ribbons they went wild with ecstasy. One young woman, Ella Roberts (nee Batey), threw her new hat in the air and to this day she still waits for it to be recovered. But as she recalls, 'it was well worth it'.

In July 1929 the Party moved into offices 'above the Liverpool and Martins Bank' in Laygate where they were to remain for over thirty years. These premises were used by the Party in a host of ways. Not only were they utilised for organisational work and as election headquarters, they were also used for lectures and classes run by such bodies as the National Council for Labour Colleges which organised courses on 'Working Class History' and similar topics.

Chuter Ede proved an assiduous MP and loyally supported the minority Labour Government of Ramsay MacDonald, but in the 1931 General Election, Ede was swept aside along with hundreds of other Labour MPs. In fact only 2 seats were returned for Labour in County Durham as the Party was almost destroyed. Ede accepted defeat as did the local Party and, re-adopting their

Executive Committee of South Shields Labour Party at opening of Labour Hall, July 1929.
Left to right, back row: Cllr R Noble, J English, W Dunn, J Kennedy, G Hudson, J Dawson, Ald A Stephenson.
Middle row: E Gompertz, Mrs Johnson, Mr McCormack, Cllr R Morgan, E Towns, G Brown, Ald G Stoker,
Mrs Bell, Ald W Pearson. Front row: Mrs Prince, Mrs Ede, Ald J Dunlop (mayor), Mrs Dunlop, Chuter Ede.

erstwhile MP, they set about rebuilding for the following election.

South Shields General Election 1931

Harcourt Johnstone (Lib)	30,528
James Chuter Ede (Lab)	20,512
majority	10,016

The Durham Miners Association had long been particularly generous to the South Shields Party. This was especially so following this electoral debacle of 1931 when 228 Parliamentary seats were lost, leaving the Labour Party with only 52 seats in the Commons. The DMA seemed to realise how precarious the Party's position was and determined to do all in its power to rectify the situation. The miners lodges were urged to play their full part and £100 was given to the South Shields Party in 1932. This generosity was repeated annually for the next thirty years. Bearing in mind that in 1932, the local Party's total income was only £258, and that was to be so for most of the 1930s, the extent of the DMA's assistance can be appreciated. The South Shields Party truly owes a great debt to the miners. They may have been slow as an organisation in fully throwing in their lot with the Party, but when they did, their commitment was total.

Early in 1931 the Party had been split with a row involving a former mayor, Alderman Curbison and Councillor Henderson the current mayor. This ended with Curbison being expelled from the Party and Henderson being asked to resign; which he did not do and continued to serve the Party faithfully for years to come. The Party nationally intervened and urged the local party to lift expulsions which it refused to do. The disagreement centred over the issue of the appointment of magistrates which consistently was a concern with the Party throughout the 1920s and 1930s and indeed is still somewhat of a sore in the 1990s. The Labour Party in South Shields a century following its inception still feels that insufficient of its members are chosen to serve on the magistrates bench.

But these internal disputes did not preclude the Party being concerned with the emergence of fascism both at home and abroad. In April 1933 the GMC passed the resolution:

'That we re-affirm our belief in Democratic Government and our determination to attain Socialism by the method of the ballot box, and believe that the British Labour and Trade Union Movement is the only safeguard against Dictatorship, we shall therefore continue to give them our wholehearted support, we express our deep sympathy with our German colleagues in their hour of agony.'

The minutes of the local party make reference to concern locally being expressed over a V Hacker described as 'a German fascist operating in South Shields'. No further information is provided about this mysterious character but clearly the local Labour activists were concerned and probably on account of anti-semitism to which the minutes often refer.

On 11 March 1934, the issue of free speech at the market place again raised its head. That the event took place against the background of dictatorship in Europe and that the person arrested, Ernie Gompertz, was a Jew, only increased the tension. But the authorities took on more than they bargained for when they arrested the resourceful Gompertz.

For generations, it had been the custom for public open-air meetings to take place at the cross under the old Town Hall in the centre of the market place, a right which the local Labour Party had utilised for over forty years. Councillor Gompertz was espousing the cause from this spot when he was arrested by Acting Inspector Patrick McManus of the Borough Police.

The fact that Gompertz was so well-known locally and held a prominent position in the town must have meant that the police officer is unlikely to have acted without higher authority. However, Gompertz with the full backing of the local Labour Party fought and won his case which as the minutes record 'safeguarded the Rights of Free Speech and Civil Liberty'. The incident provides just a hint of anti-semitic sentiment amongst the establishment in the town which can be appreciated in the context of the 1930s. It is to the credit of the local Party that they fought it so vigorously.

When the General Election was held on 14 November 1935, the mood of the country had swung back towards Labour from the National Government of the defecting MacDonald and Snowden four years earlier. The activists in South Shields saw their efforts rewarded with a convincing victory.

<u>South Shields General Election 1935</u>

J Chuter Ede (Lab)	22,031
Harcourt Johnstone (Lib)	12,932
F Burden (National)	10,784
majority	<u>9,099</u>

This was a compelling success and since that election South Shields has always been regarded as a secure Labour parliamentary seat.

The Party built on this victory at the local level and gradually increased their numbers on the Borough Council with Bill Blyton being elected at Tyne Dock in November 1936. The following year the Party took control of the council for the first time; taking a number of seats unopposed. The position was close; with the composition of the council being Labour 30, Moderate 27 and Independent 2. The Party, however, under Gompertz's guidance, was able to consolidate its hold and retained control of the council throughout the war years.

Within the Party, interest continued to be maintained in international affairs. Throughout the mid-thirties, the local party frequently debated the Spanish Civil War. The majority was always in favour of the Republican Government but initially there were some minority views that the Government was only a communist front and therefore should be opposed. However, this view waned as the conflict developed and support for the Republicans gradually grew. In October 1938, great efforts were made by activists to collect 410 tins of food which were sent to Spain. Then, on 15 January 1939, members of the local party travelled to the City Hall, Newcastle to a massive demonstration in the Republican cause at which their MP, Chuter Ede, was one of the principal speakers along with their future MP, Arthur Blenkinsop.

The advent of hostilities in 1939 with Hitler's Germany did not cause splits in the local party as had been the case in 1914. The fight against fascism united both the ideological left and pragmatic right. The lessons of Spain in the 1930s had been well understood.

Therefore, throughout World War Two, the Party gave support to the war effort. When the USSR entered the war, a number of local activists formed the Anglo-Soviet Committee in April 1943. Domestically they reacted with horror to a suggestion that there might need to be a coalition government after the war for the memories of the 1931 national government had burned deeply.

In July 1943, the Party again exhibited its tolerance and concern for others when it passed a resolution:

'that we call upon the Government to adopt the boldest possible measures of rescue of Jews from the Nazi terror and to provide shelter for refugees in suitable territory under British Control.'

By September 1944, the local Party was confident enough of the outcome of the War to again return to the international theme by 'affirming its belief in the principle of establishing a United Socialist State of Europe...'

This unanimous support of the war by the local activists was reinforced by their own personal experiences. The home front was no soft-option in South Shields which suffered grievously. The German bombers targetted the shipbuilding areas with devastating effect. In all, these raids resulted locally in 156 people being killed, 21 people seriously hurt, 3,147 people made homeless and many premises damaged including the historic market-place. Furthermore, South Shields lost more men proportionately through enemy action at sea than any other town in Britain.

Thus not surprisingly, following the hostilities, Chuter Ede comfortably retained the Parliamentary seat on 5 July 1945.

South Shields General Election 1945

Rt Hon J Chuter Ede (Lab)   22,410
Donald Parry (Nat Lib)   15,296

majority   7,114

Chuter Ede was appointed by the Prime Minister, Clement Attlee, to the Cabinet as Home Secretary, a post he held for the duration of the two Labour Governments from 1945-51.

CHAPTER FOUR

A Power in the Town: 1945-1964

However, his victory at 1945 was not as convincing as the outstanding results for Labour in other parts of the country. That South Shields had bucked the trend to some extent was reflected in the November municipal elections when 9 seats were lost and hence control of the Council. Although another factor may have been that Labour had controlled the council continuously since 1937 during which time unpopular decisions had sometimes to be taken. The following year, however, the Party took 12 seats out of 15 and regained power by a majority of two.

At a national level, the Labour Government of 1945 pressed ahead with its policies of reform. There was general acclaim in South Shields for the introduction of the Welfare State and particularly the National Health Service. There was also support from the industrial constituency for the measures of nationalisation and especially of the coal mines with so many miners living in the district; 1 January 1947 which saw the setting-up of the National Coal Board was truly a red-letter day for many.

The Labour Government in partnership with the local authority struggled with post-war shortages and bomb-damage to rebuild the town and especially to make good the shortage of homes. Unemployment was still a problem and the Party cooperated with the local Ministry of Labour in tackling the problem. However, in local elections the Party began to suffer defeats and narrowly lost control to the Ratepayers Party in 1950. Faced with this, under the supervision of Gompertz, they continued with the propaganda work from their base in Laygate.

With the Labour Government completing its programme and with its own MP serving in the Cabinet in the key role of Home Secretary, more and more of the Party's attention was turned to municipal affairs. National speakers did address meetings in the town in the late 1940s and early 1950s including the Chief Whip, William Whiteley and Michael Foot. Nevertheless, this national activity was in essence merely a diversion from the bread and butter political issues which centred upon the local council. This was accompanied by arguments and controversies often involving local personalities. The philosophy of the Party, to encourage free debate, meant inevitably that its affairs never ran completely smoothly.

In May 1949, one of the pioneers of the women's sections in the town, Mrs Mary Sutton, died. She had been a stalwart of the West Women's Section and had been instrumental in building up the strength of the section. For over forty years she had worked for the Party since she had first joined at the age of twenty-four. In addition, she had been the chair of the women's section for over twenty-five years. The Party eventually commissioned an illuminated manuscript in her memory which having extolled her services to the Labour Party continued:

'A life-long enthusiast for the Cooperative Movement, honoured in every home in Tyne Dock, loved and respected throughout South Shields, her birthplace, having brought up her children to follow her shining example...'

 gratefully commemorates
the life and work of

Mrs. Mary Sutton, for 40 years actively associated with the Labour

Party. An inspiring leader, indefatigable in service, unswervingly

loyal to principle, she was Chairman of the West Women's Section

for 25 years. The Town Council co-opted her to their Education and

Children's Committees.

A life-long and enthusiastic supporter of the Co-operative Movement,

honoured in every home in Tyne Dock, loved and respected throughout

South Shields, her birthplace, having brought up her children to follow

her shining example, she died on 3rd May, 1949, aged 64 years.

" She hath not shrunk from evils of this life,

But hath gone calmly forth into the strife,

And all its sins and sorrows hath withstood

With lofty strength of patient womanhood."

Memorial to Mary Sutton.

The memorial unveiled by Chuter Ede in January 1955 concluded:

'She hath not shrunk from evils of this life,
But hath gone calmly forth into the strife,
And all its sins and sorrows hath withstood
With lofty strength and patient womanhood'

Mary Sutton was the archetypal woman activist of the Labour Party in the 1920s and 1930s. As one reads her memorial, it is not difficult to appreciate how revered she was amongst the Party activists of the day. The Mary Suttons of Britain built the Labour Party as much as any Keir Hardie or Ramsay MacDonald.

By July 1949, there were complaints at local Party meetings that town councillors were missing many council meetings with the result that the opposition was winning votes. In an effort to improve discipline and cohesion within the Group, Labour candidates were required annually from 1955 to sign a declaration in the Party minute books which read:

'I declare my belief in the Principles of the LABOUR PARTY and agree to carry out the programme, policy and constitution on all occasions. I will attend Group meetings and act according to the decisions arrived at by the Group, and the local Labour Party.'

Individual membership of the South Shields Party was never large even in the 1920s. Most supporters deemed it sufficient to be an affiliated member through their trade union and would often play an active role in the Party by this route.

	Male	Female	Total
	Male	Female	Total
1924	80	128	208
1925	49	112	161
1926	43	128	171
1927	64	82	146
1928	52	81	133
1929	61	85	146

The number of members locally fell even further in the latter years of the Attlee Government. By 1950, attendances at Ward meetings were so sparse on occasions that it was decided to have joint meetings along the following lines:

South Joint Wards	Cleadon Park, Horsley Hill, Marsden, Harton.
West Joint Wards	Tyne Dock, Simonside, West Park, Brinkburn, Biddick Hall.
East Joint Wards	Westoe, Beacon, Hadrian, Bents.
Central Joint Wards	Rekendyke, Deans, Victoria.

As the Whiteleas estate was completed, the Party there was the exception and successfully operated as a separate ward party within the constituency Party. This arrangement was to last for over 30 years and it was not until the early 1980s that all the individual wards functioned independently.

Meanwhile, at the General Elections of 1950 and 1951, Chuter Ede was comfortably returned as MP although the latter election saw the fall of the Labour Government. This was accompanied by a renewal in the fortunes of the Party in the local elections and in 1952 it achieved sufficient gains in the council elections and then took all the vacant aldermanic seats. Although, a special meeting of the local Party had to be convened to instruct the Labour Group to take all the aldermanic seats and to do no deals with the opposition.

There was a further dispute in 1955 when two councillors voted against an issue affecting the mining industry and the Harton Lodge of the miners, led by Councillor Mackley, moved that the severest action be taken against these in addition to the 15 other councillors, including Ernie Gompertz and Vince Fitzpatrick who had abstained. However no action appears to have followed.

The 1955 General Election was a great disappointment for Labour nationally with more ground being lost although once again, Chuter Ede was comfortably returned with the help, as always, of his agent and the Party's secretary, Ernie Gompertz.

During the 1950s a number of these early pioneers of the South Shields Party died, including such stalwarts as Jack Thompson of St Hilda Miners, Charles Smith of the Boilermakers, Harry Bainbridge another miner, Mrs Scibble, Jimmy Hardwick, Richard Longstaffe and many others.

Many of the early pioneers were particularly strong characters who by their personalities and determination had overcome severe deprivation to attain high civic office. Typical of these was Charlie Smith. He had been born into poverty at Pan Bank area of the town in 1876. His family suffered repeated evictions so that Charlie later commented 'I never lived in much else than one room until I got married'. His mother went charring and as a young child Charlie had to beg for bread. Later he was forced to sell matches in the market place and undertake any other

E Gompertz and Chuter Ede, General Election, 1955.

odd jobs which were available. These experiences made the young man think there must be a better society than the one he had experienced and he became a socialist.

When he was 16 he was involved in an incident during a strike when a woman was injured. Although he denied any involvement it was to no avail and he was sentenced to a month's hard labour or a £2 fine. He could not raise the money so went to prison. Such personal injustices drove the young Smith even further into the trade union and labour movements. To be a socialist was not easy in those days and he recalled that often canvassing meant dodging showers as opponents emptied buckets of the unspeakable on them!

He spent fifty-six years working as a boilermaker in Readhead's shipyard during which time he was active in his union and on five occasions was chairman of the Tyne and Blyth District Committee. In this capacity he became a friend of George Rowe and actively supported his candidature for parliamentary honours in South Shields in 1918.

This was the year that he was first elected onto the borough council and in 1936 he became the mayor. The following year he was made an alderman and then in 1950 he became a Freeman of South Shields. When he died in May 1953 he left a legacy of social reform and was an inspiration for generations of workingmen.

Shortly before Charlie Smith's death, the town lost one of its two sons who had gone on to become Labour MPs elsewhere. Dick Ewart was born in the town in 1904 again into considerable deprivation and on leaving St Bede's School he went down the pit at Marsden. There he played an active part in the union until a rock fall left him seriously injured when he was 21, forcing him to leave the pit. After a period of unemployment he found work as a marker in a billiard hall which he later went on to manage. The young Ivor Richardson spent many hours there chatting to Dick who was widely-read and very well-informed on a wide variety of subjects. By this time he had joined the National Union of General and Municipal Workers and in 1938 became a full-time official.

At the age of 28, Dick was elected onto the local council for the Holborn Ward which he was to hold until 1943 when he retired on moving away to work. Between 1936 and 1939 he was chairman of the housing committee and did much good work in this capacity. In 1945 he was to go to Parliament as one of the two MPs for Sunderland and following the constituency being split he was elected for Sunderland South in 1950 and again in 1951.

He travelled to Spain and following the visit, in the *Catholic Herald* of 16 April 1948, he advocated Marshall Aid for fascist Spain. He argued that 'In these days when dangers are threatening the great Christian heritage, Spain should share in the Western Union'. (1) These views brought him into conflict with some of the activists in his Sunderland constituency but the arguments were well-rehearsed being reminiscent of the minority views being echoed in the South Shields Party meetings of the 1930 when the Spanish Civil War was being debated and doubts expressed about the Republican cause.

Following this controversy, he devoted most of his political energies to his native North East being elected secretary of the Northern Group of Labour MPs. In this capacity, he visited shipyards, mines and trading estates in the region and was constantly raising regional issues in Parliament. He remained a devout and active Roman Catholic all his life, fighting for social justice and fairness.

Meanwhile, as the first generation was lost, a new generation of activists came to the fore and Gompertz himself was over seventy and had become one of the elder statesmen. He had been a councillor for many years, ran the Party on strict lines, brooking no concessions and his enemies in the Party were accumulating. In a sense Chuter Ede was of a similar generation but as he was based in Surrey and was a prominent national figure he had protection by virtue of both his standing and, ironically, his remoteness.

The move against Gompertz finally came at the Party's last AGM of the 1950s. Alderman Ernie Mackley attempted to raise the issue of the chairman and secretary, but it was ruled that this could not be debated as it would require a notice of motion.

This duly appeared at a meeting of the Party on 1 March 1960 and the key part of the motion was that:

'The present post of secretary agent be abolished and a part-time secretary be elected; the Party agent to continue as full-time agent so long as authorised by the member for the Borough and the Labour Party.'

Behind this almost bland motion was the underlying motive to do away with a full-time secretary, thus destroying Gompertz's power-base. Following an acrimonious debate involving procedural matters as well as content, the motion was passed by a substantial margin of 47 to 18. The minutes simply record 'The Secretary Agent made a brief statement'. The meeting's report is then concluded with three single words, 'Good Bye, comrades' - written of course by A E Gompertz, a poignant and telling finale by a man who had served the Party faithfully for 48 years.

The extent of the majority against Gompertz was surprising and was compounded by an uncharacteristic meanness of spirit displayed by the Party members. When a motion was moved two months later that a presentation be made to A E Gompertz as a recognition of his outstanding service, it was voted that the motion be deferred for three months. When that period of time expired there was a move to extend the deferral for a further three months. On this occasion the meeting decided otherwise and recommended that Gompertz should be 'made a Freeman of the Borough in recognition of his services to the Town'.

The Labour Group which had the determining voice on the awarding of this honour did not act upon the resolution of the Party meeting, and Gompertz had to wait until 1967 before he was finally made a Freeman of South Shields. The Party did make an award of a trophy to him in 1963 but characteristically Gompertz had suggested that it be passed onto the Local Education Authority as a prize for musical attainment by schoolchildren.

To add to the drama, on the day following the crucial Party meeting there was a full meeting of the Borough Council on 2 March 1960 and Gompertz stunned the town by announcing that he was to resign not only from the Council but from all his public offices. In a statement to the press he declared, 'I have not resigned as secretary-agent, the post has been abolished and I have gone with it'. He further declared, 'One cannot live in the past - for the Party, it is the future which counts. I shall, of course, remain as an ordinary Party member'.

In this philosophical vein, after twenty-eight years as a councillor and forty-eight as a servant of the Party, 'Gompy' left the political scene. Perhaps, the *Shields*

Gazette best caught the spirit of the event when it reported:

> 'Every weekday morning for nearly 30 years a stiff, hawk-faced figure on whom time seems to have made as little impression as rain on granite, has turned his key in the lock of a dingy doorway beside a bank at the corner of Laygate and Green Street, South Shields.
>
> 'In days roaring with victory, or silent with defeat, he has pushed back the door against the wall and then, having carefully gathered up the morning's mail, mounted with the purposeful deliberation of a homing spider up the twisty flight of stairs to a poky landing on the first floor.
>
> 'There the turning of another key opens a second door, through whose grimy portals the stiff, hawk-faced figure enters briskly into a welcoming gush of fustiness. This door is very swiftly closed, and after it has snapped shut and after he has manoeuvred himself through the clutter of chairs, filing cabinets, bookcases and heaps of leaflets Mr Aaron Ernest Gompertz is nestling in the very centre of his lair.
> "Abolished"
> So it has been for almost half a normal lifetime. But in a very few days now it will not be so any more.' (2)

His departure was uncompromising as was his life in politics. He was as unbending in his beliefs as he was firm. From a family of Dutch Jews, he had been born in Middlesbrough in 1888 and moved to South Shields when he was twelve. He was a teetotaller, a non-smoker and a vegetarian. He had fought for the 'Cause' and perhaps more than any other individual shaped the South Shields Labour Party. He spoke at open air meetings, addressed cold halls and trudged the rain-soaked streets canvassing for voters. He had been in many ways the dominant political figure in the town for years. His exit marked the end of an era and it is unlikely that such a personality will re-appear in South Shields politics.

Bill Blyton, who was no mean judge of character, knew Gompertz well for over forty years and held him in the highest regard. He described him as 'incorruptible' and the 'greatest of all' the party activists of his time. He gave 'yeoman service' in building-up the Party and was 'a very great socialist, a brilliant councillor, a tenacious fighter and a formidable debater...a first-class man'.

The prime movers in removing him from his office did not take over the reins of the Party. It was left to a younger generation as the likes of Brian Howard, Jim Florence, Ken Scrimger and Liz and Murtagh Diamond to take over the responsibility.

Almost coinciding with Gompy's going was the Party's enforced move from their premises which they had rented above the bank on the corner of Laygate and Green Street for 32 years. The new leaders were determined that the Party should own their own premises. Eventually, after much searching, they decided to purchase a large victorian terraced house at 143 Westoe Road in September 1962.

In common with most other constituency Labour Parties, there was an obstacle; no money. Frantic efforts were made to raise the deposit with a number of Party members personally making loans and gifts. Mrs Elizabeth Diamond, a school headmistress, in particular devoted so much time to pursuing people for money that one active member was known to have remarked, 'if you saw Liz coming, it got to the stage that you tried to avoid her'. But it was such dedication that raised the deposit and the Party will always be indebted to Liz and her key helpers. Without her, it is unlikely that the local Party could have bought the house.

The total cost of the new headquarters to the Party was £2510-7s-4d. By September 1962 the local Party had managed to scrape together £900 and a mortgage was taken out from a building society. As it happened, the local activists managed to beat the repayment deadline and all the monies were completely repaid by 31 January 1967. After 70 years the South Shields Labour Party finally owned their own home.

But raising the money was not the only obstacle. The building itself needed attention. Not only was it a case of modernising the house but clearly it had to be adapted to suit a Party's headquarters. Here again the Party was fortunate, for among their activists were Ken Scrimger and Jim Doneghan who were in the building trade and who with others gave generously of time and expertise in adapting the house to its current usage. Since then other party members such as Alex Greig have carefully maintained and modernised the fabric of the building.

On 19 January 1963, the building was officially opened and named 'Ede House' after the sitting MP by the Rt Hon Douglas Jay MP. As it happened, drama surrounded the event. The Leader of the Opposition, Rt Hon Hugh Gaitskell MP, had been due to perform the opening but sadly was taken ill a little before and tragically died on the evening prior to the opening. This also meant that the Party's deputy leader, Rt Hon George Brown MP, who had agreed to be present when Gaitskell was originally taken ill was precluded from attending until the evening.

Mayor's Parlour, 1963.
Left to right: E Fernyhough MP, Douglas Jay MP, Bill Blyton MP, Ald P Brady (Mayor), Chuter Ede MP and A Blenkinsop.

Meanwhile, the Party had also faced another change. In July 1960, J Chuter Ede announced he would retire at the following General Election. He was 78 and had fought the constituency, with Gompertz as his agent, no less than eight times.

To some, Chuter Ede may have seemed a strange choice as the Labour representative for South Shields. When he had been originally selected in 1926, he had already had some brief parliamentary experience as an MP and was judged to be one of the Party's rising stars. One of the reasons for his selection was that it was felt that he could add an aura of respectability to the emerging local Labour Party. At the time he was seen as a man who could bring across Liberal voters to the Labour cause and this he did. Indeed, initially he had been a Liberal himself and in 1908 won a seat on the local council in Epsom where he had been born in 1882, the son of a grocer. Although he won a scholarship to Cambridge, the financial limitations of his family stopped him from completing his course and he turned to schoolteaching in his native Surrey. Politically, he saw the light early on and switched to the developing Labour Party, reflecting that radical, non-conformist tradition which has always represented such an important role in the philosophy and practice of the Party. But his approach to politics should not be seen as anything other than truly Labour. One journalist writing his obituary in 1965, misunderstood and misrepresented him and the Party when he wrote, 'he set too much store on individual liberty to be more than a cautious, pragmatic socialist.' Chuter Ede had set out in politics to fight injustice and poverty and from that course he never wavered. Towards the end of his career, after thirty-four years association with the South Shields Party, when he announced his intention in 1960 to retire, he did so by declaring, 'There are still fights for justice and freedom to be waged. Locally and nationally full employment has still to be secured and maintained'. (3)

Chuter Ede never let the South Shields Party down. He achieved everything they wished of him; he won the constituency from the Liberals and made it into one of Labour's safest seats. He represented the town not only in the House of Commons for thirty-one years but also for six years in the Cabinet, occupying one of the highest offices in the land, that of Home Secretary. He was one of Labour's most respected leaders and played a full and enthusiastic part in the social revolution which the post-war Attlee Government brought about in Britain.

What was perhaps unusual, however, was that he remained not only a man from the South but for much of his political life, whilst representing an industrial, working-class town in the North of England in Parliament, he also continued to serve in local government in the South. He sat on Epsom Urban District Council from 1908-27 and from 1933-37 was the Charter Mayor. In addition, he served on Surrey County Council from 1914-49. His trusted friend and agent, Gompertz, referred to this apparent paradox and placed it in a positive context in his own appreciation on his death by saying, 'Although a man from the South, he seemed to understand instinctively the sufferings of the North and did more than was realised to make the southern people aware of what was happening. He went to the people who counted and told them what he had seen and what ought to be done'. (4)

However, it must be remembered that the norms of political life in the 1930s and 1940s were not the same as those of the 1990s or indeed the 1890s. Furthermore, many in the 1990s judge Chuter Ede as they remember him personally; a rather severe, ex-cabinet minister who was eighty-two when he finally ceased to be MP for South Shields and became Lord Chuter Ede. Like his local ally, Ernie Gompertz, he had grown old representing the town and building-up the local party. It is much more difficult, but probably more accurate, to envisage him in 1926 as a relatively young man, passionately fighting for the miners during their long, bitter strike or thrilling the local activists by snatching victory for the first time in 1929. Few recall, for example, that in the 1926 strike, when there were only spasmodic railway services, he felt he had to come up to South Shields so he made part of the journey from Surrey by train and then completed it on foot. He was the longest-serving MP the town has had and that record is unlikely to be surpassed. He was a good man who served the town with dignity and he continued to fight against poverty and injustice right up to his death on 11 November 1965. Behind the austere, stern mask, there was kindness, tolerance and humility which few public men possess.

Perhaps the last word of assessment should be left to that son of the town, Lord Blyton, who knew him closely for almost forty years. He summed up Chuter Ede as a 'shy man with little small talk. He would pass you in the corridor of the House of Commons without speaking.' Yet in spite of that and the fact that they had served in Parliament together for twenty years and Bill had previously been on Ede's general management committee for nineteen, he concluded aptly that 'Chuter Ede had been a good MP for South Shields'. That was high praise from an old colleague.

There was obviously no hurry in finding a replacement for there were still four years of the Parliament to run. With all the disturbance of Gompertz's departure and moving the office temporarily to 29 King Street, the Party officers had their hands full.

In the autumn of 1961, the affiliated branches and wards were invited to make nominations for a prospective candidate. On 11 November 1961, six candidates were shortlisted; Arthur Blenkinsop, Ernie Mackley, W (Ted) Garrett, J Johnson, E Fletcher and D Chasworth.

The Party met on 3 December 1961, and by a large majority chose Arthur Blenkinsop with the local alderman, Ernie Mackley, being a poor second and the other candidates being 'also-rans'. Interestingly, Ted Garrett, Ted Fletcher and Jimmy Johnson went on to be MPs in Wallsend, Darlington and Hull West respectively.

Arthur Blenkinsop was well-known in the North East, as he had been MP for Newcastle East from 1945 and had been regarded as very unfortunate when he lost the 1959 General Election by 98 votes, due largely to a slum clearance programme. In the 1945-51 Labour Governments, he had been a junior minister at the Ministry of Pensions from 1946-49 and at the Ministry of Health 1949-51.

Thus, the local Party entered into the 1960s with a new regime but perhaps the final word on the old should be left to the man who had done more than any other individual to guide the Party through the previous three decades, Ernie Gompertz. At the Armstrong Hall in January 1963 he said,

'South Shields is worthy of the greatest effort and sacrifice. It is a wonderful town with wonderful people. They have been kind to me and generous to the Party. We are now the foremost political party in the town and we intend to remain so.' (5)

By those few short sentences, Gompy not only summarised the political scene in South Shields, but also

Party Officers, October 1962.
Left to right: B Howard, Chuter Ede MP, W Malcolm, E (Liz) Diamond, A Blenkinsop.

showed what a 'big' man he was. The undoubted harsh treatment he had suffered at the hands of his comrades was put behind him as he illustrated the special bond which had grown-up between himself and the town.

CHAPTER FIVE

A New Era: 1964-1992

Arthur Blenkinsop entered the political arena in South Shields at a period of great change. The secretary-agent had gone, the premises had been lost and Chuter Ede after over 30 years of service was going. Ken Scrimger agreed to act as his agent and together they worked to make the transition as smooth as possible.

The Party used the years of shake-up to advantage. The new headquarters acted as a stimulus, helped them to forget the tribulations of the changes and members entered the 1964 General Election campaign with optimism. They were able to turn the upheaval into advantage as the Party's national theme was the 'need for a change' after '13 wasted years'. Harold Wilson had caught the nation's mood and the result was the return of a Labour Government with a narrow majority of four.

Locally the result was encouraging, with Labour's majority increasing from 8,939 in 1959, to 13,350. It was a happy time. Stimulated by the narrow majority nationally, the Party remained united and determined, and when another General Election was called in March 1966, Arthur Blenkinsop further increased his majority to 14,489.

In the months following his initial narrow victory in 1964, Harold Wilson had held the imagination of the British people. It was a touch he carried over following his overwhelming electoral victory in 1966. Much progress was made in educational and social spheres with liberal reforms heralding the 'swinging Britain' era. However, trouble was brewing on the economic front as the Labour Government struggled to deal with the inherited balance of payments problems. The response of cuts in public services brought dismay to many Party members and the introduction of a prices and wages policy brought the party and trade unions into conflict both nationally and locally.

As the 1960s drew to a close, the Labour Party and the TUC nationally decided that joint trades councils and labour parties were not sensible and a decision was taken to sever the formal links. Furthermore, tensions had been developing both locally and nationally and it was felt that each body would be stronger if operating separately. Thus at the AGM of the joint body in South Shields on 17 February 1970 it was resolved:

'That South Shields Labour Party and Trades Council be disbanded as a joint organisation, as at present constituted...Recommend the establishment of two completely separate new organisations, namely;
a) The South Shields Constituency Labour Party
b) The South Shields Trades Union Council.'

This resolution was passed and twelve months later, on 25 February 1971, after fifty-three years of joint working, the two bodies finally separated although the TUC continued to rent offices in Ede House for a further ten years before they left on obtaining alternative accommodation.

Following a few difficult years the Government's policies began to succeed and the balance of payments issue was finally overcome. Arthur Blenkinsop had loyally supported the Government and in the process had endured many a contentious debate locally. In the early summer of 1970, the opinion polls were favourable to Labour and an election was called for 18 June 1970.

Once again the election in South Shields was a victory for Labour. Nationally, however, confidence in the Government was extremely fragile and in the course of the campaign, the Conservative leader capitalised on public concern over the cost of living by promising to 'cut prices at a stroke'. Events turned sour for the Party and a Conservative Government headed by Edward Heath MP was elected. This administration began to reverse some of Labour's achievements and implement alternative Tory policies. Fairly soon this brought the Government into conflict with organised labour in the work place.

Ironically, the Tory policies split the Labour Party which, not having recovered from the trauma of some of its own Government's decisions, was not able to respond purposefully to the new challenges. Some issues were easy enough. When the Government attempted to coerce the National Coal Board into restricting miners wages, the party in South Shields and nationally, threw in its support for the NUM. Similarly, when the Education Secretary, Margaret Thatcher MP, took away school milk from secondary school children, the South Shields Party, with its memories of TB and rickets, responded with anger. Other issues, however, were not so clear-cut.

One issue promoted by the Conservative Government which caused great consternation within Labour's ranks was that of the European Economic Community, or Common Market as it was then called colloquially. Edward Heath had negotiated entry and on 28 October 1971, placed a motion before the House of Commons for ratification. The Parliamentary Labour

Party officially decided to vote against and the vast majority of Labour MPs, including David Clark who then sat for Colne Valley, did so. However, a number of pro-European MPs defied the whips and voted for ratification, amongst them Arthur Blenkinsop.

Some delegates to the GMC objected and three resolutions criticising the MP were submitted from trade union branches. The South Shields Party like the national one was split on this matter and it was agreed to hold a special meeting with the MP present to thrash out the issue. Arthur explained to the GMC on 14 November that he had always been pro-European and at his adoption meeting had made that 'quite clear'. He claimed his vote was only on the principle and that he too rejected the Tory terms. A heated debate followed and in the end the majority of the GMC took a different view from their MP. A resolution was passed seeking 'assurances from their MP with regard to his future conduct in divisions where the whip is applied'. The MP gave the necessary assurances and many of those present, although disagreeing with his stance, were impressed by the sincerity and dignity with which he explained his actions.

This was one of the very few instances of the local Party being so at odds with its sitting MP that it felt it necessary in essence to reprimand him. However, it was an issue which was to split the Party right across Britain. The majority was against entry to the Common Market in the early 1970s and it is interesting to contrast the vote of the South Shields Party towards the end of the Second World War in September 1944 when it was in favour of establishing a united socialist state of Europe.

However, the issue which caused greatest consternation in South Shields was the Housing Finance Act of 1972 which forced local authorities to increase council house rents dramatically. There was unanimity in opposition to the proposals but a split came when a response by the elected council had to be determined. Some felt that they had been elected on a platform to keep rents low whilst others felt it their duty to follow the national policy of implementing the 'law of the land' but of mitigating its effects wherever possible.

Initially, a number of local councillors opposed implementation, and some transferred their worldly chattels to their spouses in case of surcharging. As the weeks went by, one by one the numbers reduced until there was only a handful of renegades. One of the most adamant was Cllr Jim Davison, who resigned his council seat, forcing a vacancy in Biddick Hall ward, which he then contested again on the basis of reluctant implementation of the Act, winning in an overwhelming manner. Thus the Act caused much heart-searching and any decision went against the grain. A number of Party activists could not take it and dropped out of political activity altogether. However, Jim Davison's action in resigning and seeking a fresh mandate served to clear the air somewhat.

Another piece of legislation which caused much disquiet in the South Shields Labour Party was the Local Government Act of 1972 which reformed the structure of local government. It proposed a two-tier system based on districts and counties. Since its incorporation in 1850, South Shields, although geographically in County Durham, had been a county borough meaning that all functions of local government were the responsibility of the one council. The new Act hit at this unitary principle in two ways. First, it meant that South Shields had to share some of its functions such as transport and fire, with a wider authority, Tyne and Wear. Secondly, it amalgamated South Shields Council with those of Boldon,

Hebburn and Jarrow, into a new district council of South Tyneside. Not surprisingly, there was near unanimity in opposition to this proposal, but in spite of this, the reforms went ahead.

In 1973, elections were held for the embryonic new authorities which worked as shadow administrations until they became full legal entities in 1974. In these initial elections the local Labour candidates won 6 of the 9 county seats and 21 of the 39 district seats. A new chapter of local government began. Councillor Vincent Fitzpatrick, a stalwart of the South Shields Party and a man of great integrity and ability, was elected leader and he led the transition from the four local bodies into the one homogeneous authority. He remained leader with distinction until 1990. Without his wise counsel and political skill, the difficulties of the new local government unit would have been much worse. He was highly respected in wider local government circles and his death on 12 February 1992 left a huge void in the local party.

By the end of 1973, the Tory government had so mishandled the economic and industrial situation that they were forced to introduce a three-day working week with the consequential hardships in lost production and wages. Once more they were locked into a battle with the miners who were ultimately to prove successful again. This confrontation forged unity within Labour ranks in South Shields and thus they entered into the General Election of February 1974 in high optimism.

Their mood was justified and following a good local and national campaign, Labour was to return victorious once more. Harold Wilson was able to form a minority Government which managed to struggle on until October 1974, when a slightly better result was achieved, allowing the formation briefly of a majority Government. The

Prime Minister had achieved the enviable record or winning four general elections as leader of the Labour Party.

The two elections of 1974 in South Shields produced a new and unpalatable feature, the presence of a candidate from the extreme right-wing party, the National Front. Fighting on a platform akin to that of the neo-fascists throughout Europe it emphasised the problem of immigration and attempted to whip up the race issue. In all the previous 18 Parliamentary elections in the town since 1832, there had never been an extreme right-wing candidate. The local Labour Party, which had always expressed a liberal approach to race matters, responded with vigour. The electors showed their tolerance and good sense and in the October election they gave Arthur his largest majority.

South Shields General Elections 1974

	February	October
A Blenkinsop (Lab)	30,740	26,492
N S Smith (Con)	18,754	11,667
L Garbutt (Lib)	---	8,106
W Owen (Nat Front)	1,958	711
majority	11,986	14,825

Arthur Blenkinsop had intimated, following the February election, that he intended that to be his final Parliamentary contest as he had fought every one since 1945. In view of the closeness of the national result and the imminence of another election he was persuaded to stand again. As soon as that success was behind him, Arthur reiterated his intention, and in the early summer of 1975 the local party agreed on a timetable to select a replacement. A formal announcement appeared in the national Party's newspaper, *Labour Weekly*, in August 1975.

The local party were very open and in spite of there being several local hopefuls, they invited any aspiring candidates to submit their names. Then, for several evenings, long meetings of party members were held at Ede House when potential candidates were invited to address the meeting for five minutes and then answer questions for a similar period. Following this, the local ward and trade union branches made their formal nominations.

By the time the selection conference took place in November 1975, six candidates had been short-listed - none of them from the town - David Clark, Harry Cowans, Ken Eastham, John McWilliam, Jack Miller and Michael Wedgeworth. As had been the case in the previous selection conference of 1961, four of the six went on to become MPs; Cowans in Newcastle Central, Eastham in Manchester Blackley and McWilliam in Blaydon. But it was David Clark who was given the honour of bearing Labour's green and white colours in South Shields.

David had only just lost the Parliamentary seat of Colne Valley the previous year, which he had gained from the Liberals in 1970. The son of a gardener, he had left school in Cumbria at 16, to work on the land as a forest worker before being employed in a textile mill. By night-school studies he gained the qualifications to enter university in Manchester and became a University lecturer before entering Parliament at the age of 30 in 1970. He already had links with the North East: his grandfather was a miner at Washington colliery and his mother was born in Sunderland. Whilst in Parliament he had become one of the foremost advocates of environmental issues making his maiden speech on acid-rain. In 1972 he had been appointed onto Labour's front-bench as agriculture spokesperson.

Throughout its existence, one of the perennial problems has been differing views between sections of the Party. In spite of the establishment of a formal Labour Group on the council with clear standing orders, difficulties continued to occur sporadically. Towards the end of 1977, potentially one of the most serious rifts occurred. Proposals to establish a sixth-form college in the town were debated in the council and the Labour Group had in effect decided to oppose the idea with the result that eight of South Shields' councillors disobeyed the whip; Cllrs J Davison, Liz Diamond, M Diamond, V Fitzpatrick, G Graham, L Jordison, W Malcolm and K Reid. Three of the rebels agreed to obey future decisions of the Group on the issue, the remaining five had the whip withdrawn from them. The GMC of the local Party was most enthusiastic about the college and backed the five rebels. A stalemate was reached with the local Party in conflict with the Group. Eventually, after much negotiation, representatives of the National Executive Committee allowed a compromise to be reached in the spring of 1978 and the five councillors had the whip re-instated. Twelve years later, a similar incident occurred, again over an educational issue, which resulted in seventeen South Shields councillors being expelled from the South Tyneside Labour Group. Once more the GMC overwhelmingly backed the rebels and eventually an accommodation was again reached and the whip restored to the councillors. Just two examples of tensions emerging within the Labour movement.

Meanwhile, Arthur and David worked in tandem for the four years prior to the next election in May 1979. This was of considerable value for it meant that the new

Handing in nomination papers, 1979 General Election.
Left to right: Arthur Blenkinsop, Christine Clark, David Clark, Lord Blyton.

candidate was familiar with the problems and the personalities of the town by that time. A short and vigorous campaign then ensued with the following result.

South Shields General Election 1979

David Clark (Lab)	28,675
R G Booth (Con)	15,551
L W Monger (Lib)	6,003
majority	13,124

Within a month of the General Election, the Party had to face its first Euro-election. Following the confirmation of Britain's entry to the European Community and that body developing some democratic institutions, elected Members of the European Parliament were required. South Shields was joined together with the other parliamentary constituencies of Blaydon, Gateshead West and East, Jarrow, Sunderland North and South and Tynemouth to form the South Tyne and Wear Euro-Constituency. In 1978, Joyce Quin, from across the Tyne in North Shields, was chosen as candidate and in June 1979 she was elected as the district's first MEP. Joyce was an admirable choice and with her abundant energy, did much to weld together the Euro-constituency. Furthermore, she gradually persuaded the majority of Party members, who had voted against Britain's entry to the EC, that the European Parliament had an important role to play. Joyce had a well-established Labour pedigree, with a grandfather who had helped form the North Cumberland Labour Party and a mother who was a stalwart in the Labour women's movement. She herself had worked full-time as a research officer at the Party's headquarters in London. In 1987 she was elected as the MP for the nearby Westminster constituency of

Gateshead East and in 1989 stood down from the European Parliament.

Her place was taken by Alan Donnelly who hailed from the adjacent Jarrow constituency. He had been a South Tyneside councillor and was the full-time national finance officer of the General, Municipal and Boilermakers Union. He proved a worthy successor to Joyce and through his energy and ability was able to consolidate the role of the Euro-party. Alan had a swift rise to power as he was immediately elected as secretary to the British Group of Labour MEPs in his first session. As such he did much worthwhile work, especially in building a bridge between his organisation in Europe and the Parliamentary Labour Party in Westminster.

Sadly, Arthur Blenkinsop's well-earned retirement was all too short, for on 23 September 1979 the news reached South Shields that their former MP had died. Apparently, he had collapsed whilst doing what he loved, rambling in beautiful, open countryside; this time near Sanquar in Dumfriesshire. Born in the small Northumberland village of Haydon Bridge, where his father was stationmaster, Arthur developed a deep and lasting love of the countryside and much of his political life was devoted to preserving the British landscape and trying to ensure that all had access to it. During his career he had been president of the Ramblers Association and for many years served on the executive of the National Trust. He was an early environmentalist; representing that green trait of socialism which has always had an important role in the British Labour Party.

The loss of his Newcastle East Constituency in 1959 had not only been a heavy personal blow to him but it cost him dear politically. His association with the constituency had been a long one for he had been selected as its parliamentary candidate before the Second World War when he was still in his twenties. Throughout the war, during his service in the army, he had kept in touch and it appeared a solid political base. It was just unfortunate for him that the 1959 election came when the constituency was in a state of flux following a massive slum-clearance scheme.

Following the Labour Government's loss of office in 1951, Arthur had moved up the promotional ladder within the parliamentary party and by 1959 was the official spokesman on health matters. Had he not lost his seat in 1959, he could have confidently expected to have been elected to the parliamentary party's ruling body, the Shadow Cabinet, and subsequently into Harold Wilson's cabinet in 1964. By one of those cruel tricks of politics, it was not to be.

During his second period in parliament between 1964-79, he played a constructive and active role as a backbencher; using his front bench experience to great effect. He felt it his duty to loyally support the leadership with two exceptions. He could not bring himself to vote against Britain's entry to the EEC in 1971 and later in 1977, he had severe doubts over the Labour Government's proposals to create a Scottish Assembly although in this instance he subordinated his personal views to those of the party.

Arthur was one of the kindest men in the House of Commons and had a reputation for helping and encouraging young men and women to enter the political arena. In the Commons, he had won respect from both sides of the House, for his knowledge, integrity and sincerity. His affection for his native North-East dominated his political life in his later years and he was held in the highest esteem not only by his constituents but throughout the region as was witnessed by the massive turnout at his funeral. He was deceptive in the sense that the gentle demeanour hid a man of strong and deeply-held socialist beliefs and convictions.

The 1979 result in South Shields was particularly satisfactory in view of the position nationally which saw the Labour Government, now led by Jim Callaghan, swept from power by Britain's first woman Prime Minister, Margaret Thatcher. She had offered a very radical right-wing programme which David Clark warned would take Britain back to the 1930s on many social and industrial issues, a prophecy which was ridiculed by the editor of the *Shields Gazette* but which tragically has proved to be correct.

Some of the new government's policies, such as the enforced sale of council houses, which caused such anguish in many Labour councils, was approached with more equanimity in South Shields where the arguments had been rehearsed about 60 years previously in the 1920s. But there was objection to the size of the discounts and even greater hostility to the fact that the local councils would no longer be permitted to provide replacements.

Housing was dear to the heart of the local party. From its very inception it had railed against the poor housing in the Borough and had sought to rectify the situation. As early as 1965, it could boast of 10,000 council houses in the town and by the end of the decade, the Biddick Hall, Brockley Whins, Marsden, Simonside and Whiteleas Estates had been virtually completed. By 1977, the South Tyneside Borough Council was building 700 houses a year and seemed well on course to resolving the housing problem in the area. But Thatcher's election saw the end of that dream and in 1992 there were nearly six thousand people on the council house waiting list in South Shields with no new council houses being built.

Along with housing, unemployment is an emotive issue in South Shields. In the 1980s unemployment began to rocket far above the already historic high levels. This unemployment was fanned by the redundancies in the river-related work of shipbuilding and repairing. The new Government immediately began implementing its policy of privatisation and targetted the ship-building industry which had only been taken into public ownership in 1977. Sadly, privatisation for the shipyards meant closure.

In July 1982 the town was stunned by the news that one of the most renowned shipyards in the town was to close. The yard had a world-wide reputation and its closure struck at the very heart of local pride. In turn, however, it posed a real dilemma for the local party members who were forced to choose between their pragmatic judgement and their political philosophy.

A so-called 'workers cooperative' was proposed by management and workforce (but not the unions) and it might have been expected that the local party would have backed it, as it had cooperatives in other fields. However, the Shields MP, David Clark, and the local activists examined the scheme in detail before rejecting it on the grounds that it was not viable and was underfunded. They decided to let their heads rule their hearts - a judgement which was later to be vindicated.

By one of those strange quirks of politics, there was a role reversal with the Conservatives supporting the workers cooperative. The argument rumbled on and overspilled into the 1983 General Election Campaign. The traditional Labour eve-of-poll meeting at the Town Hall almost broke-up in disarray in front of the TV cameras as the men from Readheads vented their anger and hostility against their union and Labour MP.

Following another Conservative victory nationally, Readheads re-opened in October 1983, when the Industry Minister, later to be Chancellor of the Exchequer, Norman Lamont MP, officially performed the opening ceremony. Initially, the Government did assist the company, granting them clearance to handle Royal Navy ships and HMS Ardennes came in for a refit. But, with the election behind them, the Conservatives began to lose interest and in March 1985, Readheads went into voluntary liquidation with a deficit of £448,000. The shipyard closed and much of the hard-earned savings of the workforce went with it. It is hard to envisage a more hard-faced and callous piece of political treachery than this by the Conservatives.

On Tyneside generally, the aftermath of the Falklands War did provide some brief impetus for the shipyards but it was to be all too short-lived. The government pressed ahead with its privatisation plans and in February 1984, a management buy-out created Tyne Shiprepair Ltd which took over Brigham and Cowan's yard and Middle Docks in South Shields. There was a brief flurry of activity before, in June 1986, the company transferred its remaining workforce to Wallsend and closed its operations in South Shields. After centuries of shipyard work in the town, by the beginning of the 1990s only the small yard of Tyne Dock Engineering remained. Sadly, thousands of river related jobs have gone, further exacerbating the woeful unemployment position. The local Labour council fought valiantly to retain a shiprepair presence in the town but to no avail as the temporary spirit of laissez-faire Thatcherism was all pervading at the time.

The General Election of 1983 was little short of a disaster for Labour nationally with the Party achieving a mere 27.6% of the votes cast; the lowest percentage since 1918. The Conservatives used all the power of jingoistic fervour to their advantage and doubtless comparisons with 1918 could be made. Furthermore, a number of prominent Labour MPs, led by its former deputy leader, Roy Jenkins, had left the Labour Party and taken with them some activists to form the Social Democratic Party (SDP). No-one of any significance from the local Party defected but the new party had a following with the electorate. An alliance was formed with the Liberal Party nationally, and as a result the Liberals did not contest South Shields but left it open for the SDP.

Locally, there had been changes in Parliamentary boundaries since 1979, with almost 9,000 votes being transferred from South Shields to Jarrow. These electors were from the Biddick Hall and part of the Marsden Wards which had been amongst the strongest Labour areas in the town. Nevertheless, the local party ran an energetic campaign and, given the difficulties, achieved an adequate albeit disappointing result.

South Shields General Election 1983

David Clark (Lab)	19,055
P J Groves (Con)	12,653
P J Angus (SDP)	9,288
majority	6,402

The re-elected Conservative Government formed its second consecutive administration. Unemployment in the town increased towards the levels of the 1930s. At the depth of the recession in May 1986 the official unemployment rate was 23.5% with male unemployment at a staggering 27.4%. The local council and MP worked together to mitigate the worst effect of the recession but it continued to devastate the local economy.

In 1984, the Tory Government, buoyed with their second successful election and having beaten various trade union challenges, decided it was time for them to teach the NUM a lesson. In spring 1984, not the most auspicious time for miners, with demand falling and stockpiles high, the Government precipitated an industrial dispute leading to a strike by miners.

The die was cast. The miners, confident of their success following the 1972 and 1974 strikes, felt they could win. Thatcher was equally determined. No quarter was to be given. Pickets were posted outside each colliery. The flying pickets of the 1974 strike were negated by police efforts, physically restricting the movement of miners. Local miners supported by sympathetic local unions and Labour parties were left to struggle on. Miners' wives came into their own as support groups and for months the struggle continued until a year later the miners tasted defeat.

In South Shields the national scene was replicated. A hut was erected on the pavement outside Westoe Colliery gates - named by a miner with a sense of humour 'Liddle House on the Prairie' after the police inspector in charge named Liddle. The inspector became infamous by, on one occasion, ordering the police to charge down the street knocking aside bystanders and pensioners. It was a long bitter dispute which the miners, although defeated, came through with dignity.

Perhaps the most important symbolic battle came over the Plessey's factory in South Eldon Street, the largest private employer in town. This was a modern factory in the forefront of micro-technology and an extension of it had been opened only recently by the Conservative Secretary of State for Trade and Industry, Sir Keith Joseph MP. The factory was the epitome of the so-called bright future of North East industry. The company announced its proposals on 12 January 1984 to transfer the factory's functions to Merseyside. The trade unions and local councillors under the chair of the MP, determined to fight the closure. The case was taken right to the top and put to the Prime Minister, Margaret Thatcher, in a meeting with the MP, but with no success.

The MP, on the strength of the one share held by the Tyne and Wear County Council, attended Plessey's AGM in London and amidst a hostile audience of shareholders and chairman, argued on behalf of the town's factory. David Clark said it was the most 'hostile meeting I have ever addressed'. Meanwhile, meetings were being held between the MP and overseas businessmen in an attempt to find a buyer for the factory but all to no avail.

On the 4 July 1984 a historic event occurred in South Shields. At noon, the workers at Plesseys, who throughout had not taken any strike action, downed tools for two hours and attended a mass meeting immediately outside the precincts of the factory. This was addressed by prominent councillors, trade unionists and the MP. Other workers throughout the town had been invited to stop work in sympathy. The local bus drivers took their buses out of service and for two hours South Shields was virtually closed down in protest.

But, all was not lost. Although the company did move out, they were persuaded to sell part of their operation, specialising in the manufacturing of micro-circuits, to a private buyer. It had been an historic struggle on behalf of the people of the town, the likes of which is unlikely to be repeated.

Following the 1983 General Election and buoyed by the Plessey fight, the local party witnessed an upturn in its fortunes. Membership, which had traditionally been low in South Shields, began to revive. At the time of the 1975 parliamentary selection conference it stood at a little over one hundred; by 1985 this had grown to 236, by 1987 to 332 and in 1991, 572 individual members were fully paid-up.

The 1987 General Election, saw David Clark, who had been elected to the Shadow Cabinet as Shadow Environment Protection Minister the previous year, retain the seat with a doubled majority of 13,851. As the new Parliament resumed, David Clark was re-elected to the Shadow Cabinet each year from 1987 undertaking the Food and Agriculture portfolio, and from 1992, Defence.

On the local council, the reinvigorated Party began to consolidate its electoral gains. With the increased membership, seperate organisations were established in each ward of the town for the first time for almost forty years. Wards which had been regarded as virtually hopeless returned Labour councillors. In May 1987, local election day saw all ten South Shields Wards fall to the Party. This was repeated in 1988 and in 1990, when a red-letter day in the Party's history occurred and all thirty of the Town's councillors were Labour. Ninety eight years following the election of the first Labour councillor, a clean sweep had been achieved. The pioneers would have been proud.

South Shields was unusual in the North-East of England in that it had a significant number of black residents. Many of these families went back several generations and had come to the town as seamen. Although there had been some racial troubles in the economic depression of the 1930s, there was generally much more racial harmony than elsewhere. In the 1970s and 1980s, these original black families, often from the Arab States of the Gulf, were augmented by newcomers from such countries as Bangladesh. In the May elections of 1991, the first black candidate for the council, Syed Hussain, was successfully elected for Beacon and Bents.

Shortly after the 1987 General Election, across the front page of the *Shields Gazette* of 26 October was emblazoned the sad headline, "Lord Blyton is Dead". Thus the town learned that probably her greatest son had died the previous day. Bill, as he preferred to be called, had come a long way from that day on 2 May 1899 when he had been born at 75 Bowman Street in the High Shields district of the town. His father was a labourer at Cookson's white lead works across the river at Howdon. Although Bill was a bright child at Holy Trinity and Dean Road Schools and passed to go to the High School, money was not available, so he left school at fourteen. Two days later he started work at the screens at Harton Colliery, working six days a week for ten pence (10d) a day. Little did he dream that he was beginning a career which would take him from pit-boy to Parliament to peer of the realm. After six months on the surface, he moved underground as a trapper and progressed to pony-driver and then putter.

Following the outbreak of war, Bill became fed-up with working in the wet coalseams and at the age of sixteen and half he joined the Royal Navy as an ordinary seaman. No sooner had he completed his training than he found himself at Gosport and 'volunteering' for service on submarines. As Bill later recalled, he did not really volunteer and certainly not out of bravery but simply because he 'was terrified of the captain'. So within six months of working under South Shields digging coal, he found himself under the sea fighting the Germans!

In January 1919, he was demobbed from the navy and went back down the pit. Within twelve months he found himself again working in a wet area but the overmen refused to pay 'wet-money' which the hewers and putters felt they were due. Bill led a strike which turned out to be successful. It coincided with the annual lodge meeting of December 1919 and the men elected him to be the delegate to the DMA council at Durham City. So began a trade union and political career which was to stretch over the next seventy years. Typically of the man, he realised his short-comings and went to see his old schoolmaster for advice which was that he should study industrial history, economics and Shakespeare. Bill followed the suggestion to good effect and to the end he could quote Shakespeare at length. Soon he was making speeches in the Market Place and during the 1921 and 1926 miners strikes he went all over the country speaking on the miners behalf. He learned the trade of oratory and anyone who heard his eve of poll speech on behalf of David Clark at the Town Hall in 1979 would vouch for this. He became chairman of the Harton Miners Lodge from 1928-41 and secretary from 1941-3.

Bill, however, quickly appreciated that his hopes and aspirations could never be realised through trade union work alone and in 1920, his lodge elected him to be their delegate to the South Shields Labour Party, a post he held until 1945: He was elected an auditor for the borough in 1927 and then in 1936 he won the Tyne Dock ward which he represented until 1945, becoming chairman of education in 1943.

His reputation spread and the DMA placed him on its parliamentary panel. When a vacancy occurred at the 1945 General Election at Houghton-le-Spring, which contained many miners, Bill was selected. Although not strictly his home town, this was the next best for the constituency surrounded Sunderland and when he first represented it, some of the outlying parts of South Shields were in it.

In Parliament, Bill put into practice his knowledge acquired over the years of reading and work. He naturally championed the cause of miners and also kept a watchful eye on naval affairs. Very briefly, between 1947-49, he was parliamentary private secretary to the Ministry of Civil Aviation, but was forced to resign for voting against the Ireland Bill. He was a member of the Council of Europe and became a staunch critic of the Common Market. When the leadership contest took place in 1963, Bill openly supported Harold Wilson and helped to deliver the trade union MPs votes to him. On his retirement in 1964, he was elevated to the House of Lords as Baron Blyton of South Shields.

Bill never lost contact with his roots or the town in which he was born and lived. Indeed, he was subject to much criticism for living in his two-bedroom council house from where he could see the remnants of Harton Colliery, although he did eventually buy this house. He was amongst the wisest of men the author has ever met and full of common sense advice. Although deprived by poverty of a good formal education, he had made up for this by private study. His knowledge was extensive and he could quote poetry and long pieces of Shakespeare and was probably the last of the old school of outdoor orators in the town. Bill was a remarkable man and a true ambassador for South Shields and the North-East. He voiced the authentic opinions of the ordinary workingman, symbolised perhaps by his attitude to the Falklands War in 1982 when, with a grandson involved in the armed forces, Bill supported the government's policy by saying 'we cannot give way or appease a fascist junta in Argentina'. (4) He was one of that school of Labour MPs from the pits of Durham, who although deprived of formal education had wisdom in their boots.

Armed with the local Government successes, the Party organised a long campaign for the period leading up to the 1992 General Election. Many of the Party workers travelled across the river to canvass in Tynemouth in the hope of ridding the whole of Tyne and Wear of the last Tory MP. Their candidate, now with shadow cabinet responsibilities, was much in demand in marginal seats elsewhere and he undertook extensive tours which took him the length and breadth of the country in addition to his work as local candidate. The attitude of electors canvassed was extremely enthusiastic and to many experienced hands reminiscent of 1966. But the Party was beguiled and in the secrecy of the ballot box the electors chose selfishness over altruism. The Conservative Party had ditched their unpopular Prime Minister, Margaret Thatcher, in November 1990 and replaced her with John Major who had less of a strident countenance. The electorate seemed to imagine that Major represented a new type of Conservatism and decided to give him a chance. Nationally, the return of another Conservative Government was a great disappointment for the overwhelming belief in the campaign was that there would be the return of a Labour Government. But it was not to be.

However, the result in South Shields saw a further swing to Labour, with the Party achieving the highest share of the total vote in any three-way campaign in its history. The result was encouraging against a national one of great disappointment. Clearly the people of the town regarded Labour as the best government to get Britain out of its economic malaise and to begin rebuilding a fairer and more just society.

<u>South Shields General Election 1992</u>

David Clark (Lab)	24,876
J Howard (Con)	11,399
A Preece (Lib Dem)	5,344
majority	<u>13,477</u>

The local activists had little time to mourn the loss of the fourth general election, for they had to begin campaigning almost immediately for local elections a month later. These elections appeared difficult. Labour was defending all the seats in South Shields and there had been considerable criticism of the local council in the *Shields Gazette.* The Conservative Government had introduced a whole series of measures which forced local authorities to make cuts in the services they provided. Even the poll-tax, the most unpopular of local taxes introduced by the Conservatives, had to be implemented by the local council who inevitably, and so unfairly, took some of the blame for it. The party worked hard but the Labour voters still seemed to be dumb-struck by the general election result and the turn-out was low. Nevertheless, the Party showed its depth of commitment and organisation, and when the count took place, Labour retained all their ten seats. Thus, with David Clark as the Labour MP, Alan Donnelly the MEP and all but one of the local councillors taking their whip, the South Shields Labour Party entered its second century in a commanding position.

Party Officers, 1992.
Left to right; Standing: Mark Walsh, Cllr Arthur Jackson, Joan Jackson, David Clark MP, Katharine Tarn.
Seated: Cllr John Temple, Edward Malcolm, Cllr Jane Branley.

CHAPTER SIX

Conclusion

If the early pioneers, who met in Brown's Cocoa Rooms in Church Way on 31 August 1892 to form a Labour Party in South Shields, were to come back today, they would hardly recognise the town. The building in which they had originally met and which was to provide their meeting place for several years has gone - destroyed by Hitler's bombs during World War Two. Admittedly, some buildings do remain. The old Town Hall in the Market Place still stands but civic business is now conducted up the hill in the new town hall built in the prosperous Edwardian times. St Hilda's Church, just across the road from the Cocoa Rooms, escaped the bombs and is as fine as ever. But the environs are very different.

As they met in 1892, they would have been able to glimpse the pit-head gear of St Hilda Colliery - closed in 1940. Some of the gear remains, partly as a monument and partly serving a useful purpose as an escape route from the new Westoe Colliery reconstructed on the sea-front in the 1950s and 1960s. The other three local collieries have closed as well, Marsden in 1968, Harton in 1969 and Boldon in 1982. Even the modern, multi-million ton a year pit of Westoe has a question mark over its very existence. Once there were thousands of miners living in the town, now there are only a few hundred. The miners from each of the pits met in their respective halls and discussed politics; Harton Lodge in Bede Street, Marsden in Imeary Street and St Hilda at 28 Maxwell Street. Those halls have gone or were sold and now the Westoe miners meet in their modern Armstrong Hall on Stanhope Road.

In 1892, if the pioneers had walked the hundred yards to the river, they would have seen scores of ships plying their trade and the shipyards would have been busy repairing them and building new ones. Now the yards, with one exception, are gone although there is some rig-work for the North Sea oil and gas fields. Only the regular passenger ferries to the Scandinavian countries maintained the tradition of centuries.

A hundred years ago, housing in the town was amongst the worst in Britain. Conditions were appalling with the resulting poor health of residents. Overcrowding was the order of the day. Catherine Cookson, South Shields born and bred and Britain's best-selling author in the 1980s and early 1990s, graphically captures the situation in many of her novels. Now, thanks to progressive housing policies of successive Labour councils, the condition of housing has improved beyond the wildest dreams of the 1892 Party members. The new estates, in spite of their shortcomings, would have seemed utopian garden developments to them.

Of course, the world has changed since 1892 when Great Britain was the unchallenged international superpower with an empire stretching to the four corners of the earth. Queen Victoria sat imperiously on the throne. Britain was stable, its aristocracy settled and businessmen were daily making fortunes. For the overwhelming majority of its citizens, Britain was different. Life for them was hard. Work was unreliable, wages low and pensions rare. Life expectancy was short and infant mortality was high.

The world has changed. Britain has changed. South Shields has changed. But changes do not just happen. They have to be worked for. The activists in the South Shields Labour Party did just that in the town and they can take credit for many of the changes that can be seen a hundred years on. The housing, the schools and health care have been brought about by their efforts and plans.

In 1892, the activists may have been ordinary men and women who worked hard for low wages. They may have been without formal education. But they had dreams and hopes. As they looked around them, they knew there had to be a better way of running society. For as well as having dreams they were essentially practical people.

They knew that utopia could not be built overnight. Right from the outset they placed their faith in democracy, believing that through discussion and debate, through the interchange of ideas, progress would be made. That has been the hallmark of the South Shields Labour Party over the century. They have always sought to run their affairs along democratic lines, encouraging free speech, respecting minority views and accepting majority decisions. It has been politics of persuasion and not politics of force or power blocs. They have always rejected the 'Tammany Hall' approach to politics.

Initially, their prime object was to use the electoral process to obtain the election of working-people onto various boards and councils. They believed that the inherent wisdom of their own people, representing their own views, would bring amelioration in the social and industrial conditions. In a sense they were not deeply ideological. They were basically 'labourist' as opposed to 'socialist'. Only as time went on did the concept of socialism become the basis of their political philosophy but even then only in a very practical manner. Their socialism was more akin to the Scandinavian type just across the North Sea than it was to the more theoretical approach.

The majority of the early pioneers were themselves trade unionists and recognised from the outset that political success would depend upon converting their fellow unionists. It was no easy task. Many of the local union leaders were committed Liberals. They were grateful that the Liberals had given them the vote and Gladstone was still revered. Gradually, the pioneers made progress but it was painfully slow. It took almost thirty years to gain the permanent affiliation of the oldest miners' lodge in the town, St Hilda's. Although a number of remarkable individual miners embraced the ILP from the earliest days, it was not until after World War One that miners went over almost en bloc. Nevertheless, once the conversion was made, the commitment was absolute. Other unions, large and small, also played their part. The boilermakers, council workers, engineers, plasterers, railwaymens, seamens, shop assistants and upholsterers unions all were early adherents to the cause. It was, however, when trade unionists went over to Labour in force after 1918 that the Party locally made the critical political breakthrough.

Their objective of electing councillors and MPs to represent their views may have made them a class party but not a highly ideological one. Many of the early councillors were drawn from the pits, the shipyards and factories and thus in one of their primary - if not the primary - objectives, success came early. Their choice of a boilermaker and a miner as their first two parliamentary candidates re-emphasises the point.

But they did interpret quite literally the motto of the Labour Party which denoted workers as being 'by hand or brain'. Joe Abbott, the second councillor was a small shopkeeper and Jimmy Curbison was the manager of the Cooperative Society's boot and shoe repair shop. Teachers have long played a critical and instrumental role in the Party, with the likes historically of Cuth Barrass and Liz Diamond. Currently, in 1992, the Party treasurer, Arthur Jackson, and the vice-chair, Joan Jackson, are both teachers. Education has always been appreciated in the South Shields Party as was illustrated by Bill Blyton's first action on becoming a young delegate to the DMA - to go to his old schoolmaster to seek advice. The choice of MPs who were sons of a grocer, a station master and a gardener, illustrates the open-minded interpretation of working people.

The Party's insistence on operating within a democratic framework emphasising free debate and discussion has in itself created difficulties and tensions. This has usually focussed on clashes between councillors or the Labour Group and the Party member or the general management committee. One can instance the disagreements between the Party and Alderman Dunlop or Councillor Henderson; the expulsion of Councillor Curbison or the 'sixth-form college' dispute of 1977/78. Even more recently, the expulsion of seventeen South Shields councillors in 1990, although all these were re-instated, serves to make the point. But these periodic disagreements have in the long-term only strengthened the local Party.

This history of South Shields Labour Party is really the story of ordinary people's struggle to help themselves whilst at the same time aiming to help others. It is a story of self-sacrifice, often unseen and normally unrecorded, usually mundane with no heroics. Yet, nevertheless, sacrifice just as great as the sensational ones of our traditional history books. Sacrifices as true and worthy as the proverbial 'widows mite'.

This has not been the story of blood and thunder - although blood has been spilt both literally and metaphorically in the cause locally. It has been a century of slog, hard work and gradual progress by thousands of ordinary men and women. And, incidentally, the tens of thousands of ordinary Shields folk who have placed their trust in the Party through the ballot box over the years.

The pioneers of 1892 would have been thrilled that for the past sixty years or so, South Shields has been proudly represented in the House of Commons by a Labour MP. They would have been incredulous that one of the town's sons, Bill Blyton, a Harton miner, would don the ermine and take his seat in the House of Lords as Baron Blyton of South Shields. They would have been delighted that 29 of the 30 councillors in the town are from the Labour ranks.

In a sense, those very achievements have justified their aspirations and struggles. In spite of all the changes that have taken place, other things remain the same. That the secretary of the Westoe Lodge of the miners union, Edward Malcolm, is chairman of the Party, that a local lad, John Temple, born and bred in the town was secretary and that the leader of the South Tyneside Council, Albert Elliott, worked at Harton and Westoe Collieries, would have re-assured them of the continuity of their ambitions. That octogenarian, Ivor Richardson, has sat on the GMC almost continually since 1929 or that Ella Roberts, herself a member of long-standing, still represents the causes of the women's section, would add any further reassurances necessary. The other trades are still represented; the boilermakers and the municipal workers and the health employees.

The story of South Shields Labour Party has been of each generation of activists building upon the success of its predecessors. It has attempted to develop local policies and solutions within the national framework. The activists of 1992 are acutely aware of this, especially following the fourth successive general election defeat. They have, however, sufficient determination, enough dedication and commitment to the struggle to protect ordinary working people and to build a better society and world.

The pioneers of 1892 and those that have followed in the tumultuous years of the twentieth century have always had dreams. It was their very greatness that they were able to rise above their awful physical conditions and miserable existence to have their lofty dreams. That is what singled them out from their fellow citizens. They were very wise people for they understood that it was useless to have pie-in-the-sky dreams for these only led to disappointment and failure. Their dreams were essentially practical, almost impossible but still feasible. Many of them have come to fruition and their very wisdom was summed up in Joe Batey's personal political statement in his poem:

'I do not want the earth. I only ask
That portion of its plenty which is mine'.

NOTES

CHAPTER ONE: INTRODUCTION

(1) J Batey, *Durham Miners' Wages*, Sword, South Shields, 1904.

(2) C Cookson, *Catherine Cookson Country*, Heinemann, London, 1986.

CHAPTER TWO: THE BEGINNINGS

(1) *Shields Gazette*, 16 December 1891; 25 April 1892.

(2) J Lawson, *A Man's Life*, Hodder and Stoughton, London, 1932, p39.

(3) *Shields Gazette*, 25 May 1892.

(4) *Workman's Times*, 16 July 1892.

(5) *Shields Gazette*, 1 September 1892.

(6) *Labour Leader*, 12 May 1894.

(7) *Ibid.*, 18 August 1894.

(8) *Ibid.*, 16 November 1895.

(9) G W Keeton, *A Liberal Attorney-General*, Nisbet, London, 1949, p81.

(10) *Ibid.*, p119.

(11) *Ibid.*, p122.

CHAPTER THREE: BUILDING THE PARTY

(1) E Shinwell, *Lead with the Left*, Cassel, London, 1981, p10.

(2) *Ibid.*, p29.

(3) D Tanner, *Political Change and the Labour Party*, Cambridge UP, London, 1990, p109.

(4) For further account see D Price, *Fighting Like Tigers*, Newcastle Polytechnic Paper, Newcastle, 1982.

CHAPTER FOUR: A POWER IN THE TOWN

(1) *Daily Worker*, 30 April 1948.
(2) *Shields Gazette*, 3 March 1960.
(3) *Ibid.*, 11 November 1965.
(4) *Ibid.*
(5) *Ibid.*, 21 January 1963.

CHAPTER FIVE: A NEW ERA

(1) *Daily Telegraph*, 27 October 1987

FURTHER READING

There are a number of books which add further
information to the life and conditions in South Shields
and which have been helpful in compiling this history.
That former daughter of the town, the best-selling author,
Catherine Cookson, has set many of her novels in the
area and provides much colour.   In particular, her
autobiographical work *Our Kate* (Macdonald, 1969) and
Catherine Cookson Country (Heinemann, 1986) provide
vivid reflections of the town, its environs and peoples since
the early years of this century.   Another useful source of
information on the conditions in the working-class
communities of the town during a similar period is Joe
Robinson, *The Life and Times of Francie Nichol of South
Shields* (Allen and Unwin, 1975).   A local figure who
eventually went on to be a professor in Japan, James
Kirkup, provides a picture of growing up in the town in the
1930s in *The Only Child* (1957), *Sorrow, Passions and
Alarms* (1959) and *I, of all People* (Weidenfeld and
Nicolson, 1988).   George Keeton's biography of W S

Robson, *A Liberal Attorney-General* (Nisbet, 1949) gives useful information on political life in the constituency about the turn of the century and J Havelock Wilson's autobiographical *My Stormy Voyage Through Life* (Cooperative Press, 1925) adds another perspective although, unfortunately, Volume II, which covers his main period in South Shields, mysteriously disappeared without trace on route to the publishers and has never appeared. More generally, George Hodgson, *The History of South Shields*, (Reid, Newcastle, 1924) provides a background history of the town. On a lighter note, yet nevertheless containing many accurate impressions and realistic characters, often based on fact, see James Mitchell, *When the Boat Comes In* (Hamish Hamilton, 1978). Mitchell's father was a long-time Labour councillor in the town being elected in 1923 and becoming mayor 1944-45.

The Minutes of the South Shields Labour Party from 1912-51 are on microfilm, published in a series entitled *Origins of the Labour Party*, (EP Microform, Wakefield, 1979).

In addition, further information was provided to the author in interviews with Margaret Sutton (1978); Connie Lewcock (1979); Lord Blyton (1981); John Murtha (1983); Ella Roberts (1992), Ivor Richardson (1992) and Hardie Mann Blatchford Henderson (1992).

APPENDIX A

SOUTH SHIELDS ELECTION RESULTS

Election	Electors	T'out	Candidates	Party	Votes	%
1885	11,928	60.3	J C Stevenson	L	4,064	56.5
			W D Seymour	C	3,128	43.5
					936	13.0
1886			J C Stevenson	L	Unopposed	
1892	13,259	67.3	J C Stevenson	L	4,965	56.6
			H H Wainwright	C	3,958	44.4
					1,007	11.2
1895	14,307	69.8	W S Robson	L	5,057	50.7
			H H Wainwright	C	4,924	49.3
					133	1.4
1900	16,033	72.0	W S Robson	L	7,417	64.3
			R Readhead	C	4,119	35.7
					3,298	28.6
1906	18,106	72.6	Sir W S Robson	L	9,717	73.9
			A R Chamberlayne	C	3,431	26.1
					6,286	47.8
1910 (J)	18,320	76.1	Sir W S Robson	L	9,090	65.2
			R E L V Williams	LU	4,854	34.8
					4,236	30.4
1910 (by-elec)	18,320	70.1	Rt Hon R Rea	L	7,929	61.8
			R E L V Williams	LU	4,910	38.2
					3,019	23.6
1910 (D)			Rt Hon R Rea	L	Unopposed	
1916 (by-elec)			C A Cochrane	L	Unopposed	
1918			J H Wilson	Tu-Coal	Unopposed	
1918	50,584	51.3	J H Wilson	TU-coal	19,514	75.2
			G J Rowe	Lab	6,425	24.8
					13,089	50.4

Election	Electors	T'out	Candidates	Party	Votes	%
1922	52,005	76.2	E A St A Harney	L	15,760	39.8
			W Lawther	Lab	15,735	39.7
			J H Wilson	N Lib	8,121	20.5
					25	0.1
1923	52,557	73.5	E A St A Harney	L	22,912	59.3
			W Lawther	Lab	15,717	40.7
					7,195	18.6
1924	53,122	75.3	E A St A Harney	L	23,171	57,9
			W Lawther	Lab	16,852	42.1
					6,319	15.8
1929	61,629	72.9	J C Ede	Lab	18,938	42.2
			Hon H B Robson	L	18,898	42.0
			W Nunn	C	7,110	15.8
					40	0.2
1931	63,697	80.1	H Johnstone	L	30,528	59.8
			J C Ede	Lab	20,512	40.2
					10,016	19.6
1935	62,847	72.8	J C Ede	Lab	22,031	48.1
			H Johnstone	L	12,932	28.3
			F F A Burden	N Lab	10,784	23.6
					9,099	19.8
1945	51,599	73.1	Rt Hon J C Ede	Lab	22,410	59.4
			D M Parry	N Lib	15,296	40.6
					7,114	18.8
1950	72,463	81.7	Rt Hon J C Ede	Lab	33,452	56.5
			J Chalmers	C	15,897	26.8
			J George	L	9,446	16.0
			F O Smith	Com	415	0.7
					17,555	29.7
1951	74,657	80.5	Rt Hon J C Ede	Lab	33,633	55.0
			J Chalmers	C	20,208	33.6
			C J Kitchell	L	6,270	10.4
					13,425	22.4
1955	74,340	71.6	Rt Hon J C Ede	Lab	31,734	59.6
			J Chalmers	C	21,482	40.4
					10,252	19.2

Election	Electors	T'out	Candidates	Party	Votes	%
1959	75,538	74.4	Rt Hon J C Ede	Lab	32,577	58.0
			J Chalmers	C	23,638	42.0
					8,939	16.0
1964	72,697	74.1	A Blenkinsop	Lab	29,694	55.2
			J Chalmers	C	16,344	30.3
			T H C Wardlaw	L	7,837	14.5
					13,350	24.9
1966	71,578	68.7	A Blenkinsop	Lab	31,829	64.7
			C M Dallas	C	17,340	35.3
					14,489	29.4
1970	75,032	66.8	A Blenkinsop	Lab	30,191	60.2
			Dr J McKee	C	19,960	39.8
					10,231	20.4
1974 (F)	71,929	71.5	A Blenkinsop	Lab	30,740	59.7
			N S Smith	C	18,754	36.5
			W Owen	NF	1,958	3.8
					11,986	23.2
1974 (O)	72,565	64.7	A Blenkinsop	Lab	26,492	56.4
			N S Smith	C	11,667	24.8
			L Garbutt	L	8,106	17.3
			W Owen	NF	711	1.5
					14,825	31.6
1979	70,566	71.2	D G Clark	Lab	28,675	57.1
			R G Booth	C	15,551	31.0
			L W Monger	L	6,003	11.9
					13,124	26.1
1983	61,924	66.2	D G Clark	Lab	19,055	46.5
			P J Groves	C	12,653	30.9
			P J Angus	SDP	9,288	22.6
					6,402	15.6
1987	60,754	70.7	D G Clark	Lab`	24,882	57.9
			M L D Fabricant	C	11,031	25.7
			Mrs M M Meling	SDP	6,654	15.5
			E G Dunn	Ind	408	0.9
					13,851	32.2

Election	Electors	T'out	Candidates	Party	Votes	%
1992	59,392	70.1	D G Clark	Lab	24,876	59.8
			J Howard	C	11,399	27.4
			A Preece	LD	<u>5,344</u>	<u>12.8</u>
					13,477	32.4

APPENDIX B

SOUTH SHIELDS LABOUR PARTY - OFFICERS

August 1892
President — Gordon Scott
Correspondence Sec — Charles H Reynolds
Secretary — W Willimont

September 1892
President — Joe Abbott
Correspondence Sec — Gordon Scott
Organiser — Charles H Reynolds

February 1893
President — Charles H Reynolds
Vice Presidents — C Richardson
H Smith
Secretary — W Willimont
Correspondence Sec — Gordon Scott
Treasurer — Mr Briggs
Committee — Mrs Reynolds
G Smith
R Brown
S Finnerly
E Hindmarsh

February 1912
President — Cllr J Curbison
Vice Presidents — G R Budd
R Morgan
Secretary — Charles Johnston
Assistant Sec — A E Gompertz
Treasurer — R Noble
Executive — Bro. Miller
Bro. Wake
Bro. Smith
Bro. Whineray
Bro. Swan
Bro. Fitzpatrick
Bro. Spence
Bro. Johnson
Mrs Towns

February 1918

Chairman	Cllr George Linney
Vice-chairman	Alf Chapman
Secretary	Cllr J R Curbison
Assistant Sec	A W Cousins
Treasurer	W Jackson

February 1992

Chairman	Edward Malcolm
Vice-chairmen	Joan Jackson
	Mark Walsh
Secretary	Cllr John R Temple
Treasurer	Cllr Arthur Jackson
Womens Officer	Cllr Jane Branley
Youth/Student Officer	Katharine Tarn

APPENDIX C

BIOGRAPHICAL NOTES
ON EARLY LABOUR COUNCILLORS

John Lisle. Councillor Laygate 1892-95. Tailor. Member of ILP. Trades Council officer.

Joseph Abbott. Councillor Tyne Dock 1893-99. Seaman, shopkeeper (tobacconist) and later publican of The Lifeboat and the General Gordon. President ILP 1893. Secretary of Fabian Society 1892.

John Thompson. Councillor Laygate 1893-96, Westoe 1898-1907. Miner, Marsden Lodge Secretary and checkweighman. Born 1859. Died 14 December 1926.

Jack Cullen. Councillor Laygate 1894-1908. Alderman 1908-1918. Miner at Marsden. Member of ILP. Born 1861. Died 19 September 1918.

Joe Batey. Councillor Laygate 1896-1899, 1901-1918. Board of Guardians 1894-1915. Miner, St Hilda Lodge Secretary and checkweighman 1896-1915. Member of ILP. President of South Shields Cooperative Society. MP Spennymoor 1922-42. Born Northumberland 4 March 1867. Died 21 February 1949.

Robert Hearn. Councillor Simonside 1905-08. Railway guard (mineral). Secretary ILP 1904.

John Richard Toll. Councillor Victoria 1906-17. Board of Guardians 1906-1913. Miner, St Hilda checkweighman. Member of ILP. Died 1917.

Jimmy Dunlop. Councillor Tyne Dock 1906-18. Alderman 1918-38. Mayor 1928-29. Shipyard worker (driller). Emigrated to Canada 1883. Returned to England and worked at Barrow in Furness and Middlesbrough before moving to South Shields in 1893. Member of ILP until 1904. Founded local branch of SDF in 1904.

Amateur cyclist. Born Erskine, Renfrewshire 13 May 1865. Died 6 December 1938.

Richard Vine. Councillor Victoria 1907-27. Alderman 1927-35. Miner, Harton checkweighman. Born 1856. Died 9 April 1935.

Joseph Howe. Councillor Simonside 1911-30. Miner at Harton. Member of Salvation Army.

Jimmy Curbison. Councillor Laygate 1911-29. Alderman 1929-45. Mayor 1925-26. J.P. 1925. Manager of South Shields Cooperative Society's boot and shoe department. Shop Assistants Union. Member of ILP. Chair of South Shields Labour Party 1912. Local methodist preacher. Born 1878. Died 26 December 1960.

Charles Allen Henderson. Councillor Simonside 1913-32. Alderman 1932-43. Mayor 1930-31. J.P. 1920. Railwayman. Secretary ASRS Tyne Dock No 1. Executive of NUR. Member of ILP. Born 29 May 1866. Died 1 May 1943.

George Henry Linney. Councillor Tyne Dock 1914-21, 1922-32. Alderman 1932-45. Mayor 1932-33. J.P. 1925. Board of Guardians 1913-19. Miner at Marsden. Chair of South Shields Labour Party 1918. Born 16 August 1869. Died 14 June 1945.

APPENDIX D

LABOUR COUNCILLORS REPRESENTING SOUTH SHIELDS WARDS 1992/93

ALL SAINTS

Robert S Haws
Albert Tate
John R Temple

BEACON AND BENTS

Gerry Graham
Syed Hussain
Audrey McMillan

CLEADON PARK

Allen G Branley
Margaret A Hamilton
Neil Maxwell

HARTON

Evelyn Doneghan
Robert Edwardson
Cecilia Pearson

HORSLEY HILL

Catherine Brown
Iain Malcolm
Shirley Stratford

REKENDYKE

Martin E Lightfoot
Beryl B Scott
John Turner

TYNE DOCK & SIMONSIDE

Michael H Clare
Arthur Jackson
Kirby W Watson

WESTOE

Jane Branley
John Hodgson
Ron Reynolds

WEST PARK

James F Harper
Philip J Lambert

WHITELEAS

William E Brady
Albert L Elliott
Robert Stidolph

APPENDIX E

BIOGRAPHICAL NOTES ON PARLIAMENTARY CANDIDATES

George Rowe *Unsuccessfully contested South Shields 1918*
Born East Ham, London 1872. Educated at Stephenson Memorial School, Willington Quay. Apprentice caulker at Palmer's Howdon Yard; Boilermaker 1891. Armaments Committee of the North East Coast 1914-18, Munitions Board 1916-18, Committee of Production 1917-18. Councillor, Collingwood ward of Tynemouth C B 1913-28, Alderman 1928-33, Chairman of Tynemouth Public Assistance Committee 1930. Chairman of Education Committee 1931-33. Order of British Empire. Justice of the Peace 1922. Died 8 March 1933.

William Lawther *Unsuccessfully contested South Shields 1922/23/24*
Son of Edward Lawther, of Choppington, Northumberland. Born 1889; married 1915, Lottie Laws (she died 1962). Educated at Choppington Colliery School, and Central Labour College, London. Elected for the Barnard Castle division of Durham in May 1929 and sat until he was defeated in October 1931. Member of Durham County Council 1925-29. Member of TUC General Council 1935-54, President 1949. Knighted 1949. President of Miners' Federation of Great Britain, later National Union of Mineworkers 1939-54. Died 1 February 1976.

James Chuter Ede *MP South Shields 1929-31; 1935-64*
Son of James Ede, of Epsom. Born 11 September 1882; married 1917, Lilian Mary (she died 1 July 1948). Educated at Epsom National School, Dorking High School, Battersea P T Centre, and Christ's College, Cambridge. School Master 1905-14; Secretary to Surrey County Teachers' Association 1919-45; member of Epsom Urban District Council 1908-27 and 1933-37, of Surrey County Council 1914-49; Vice-Chairman 1930-33, Chairman 1933-37; Honorary Freeman of Wimbledon 1937, of

Epsom and Ewell 1939, of Mitcham 1945, and of South Shields 1950; Charter mayor of Epsom and Ewell 1937; Deputy-Lieutenant and J P for Surrey; President County Councils Association 1953-61; President Commons, Open Spaces and Footpaths Preservation Society 1955-61; Parliamentary Secretary Board of Education May 1940-Aug 1944, Ministry of Education Aug 1944-May 1945; Leader of House of Commons Mar-Oct 1951. Home Secretary Aug 1945-Oct 1951. P C 1944. C H 1953. Unsuccessfully contested the Epsom division in 1918. Elected for Mitcham in March 1923 and sat until he was defeated in December 1923. Unsuccessfully contested Mitcham again in 1924. Served with East Surrey Regiment and R E 1914-18. Member of Parliamentary Labour Party Parliamentary Committee 1951-55. Created Baron Chuter-Ede (Life Peerage) 1964. Trustee of British Museum 1951-63. Deputy-Chairman of BBC General Advisory Council 1952-59. Died 11 November 1965.

Arthur Blenkinsop *MP South Shields 1964-79*
Son of John Matthewson Blenkinsop. Born 30 June 1911; married 1939, Mary Norman. Educated at Newcastle Royal Grammar School. University Research Fellow 1960-61. Parliamentary Secretary Ministry of Pensions May 1946-Feb 1949; Ministry of Health Feb1949-Oct 1951. Chairman of Committee for Social and Health Questions of Council of Europe 1968-70. Former member of Advisory Council on Drug Misuse. Chairman of Labour Parliamentary Shipping Group. Chairman Council of Town and Country Planning Association. Member Executive Committee National Trust. Sat for Newcastle East from 1945-59, when he was defeated, and for South Shields from 1964 until he retired in April 1979. Lord Commissioner of Treasury Aug 1945-May 1946. Opposition spokesman on Health until 1959. Voted in favour of entry to EEC on 28 October 1971. Died 23 September 1979.

David Clark *MP South Shields 1979-*
Son of George Clark. Born 19 October 1939; married 24 March 1970, Christine. Educated at Windermere Grammar, and Manchester University. Forest worker 1956-57; Laboratory Worker in Textile Mill 1957-59;

Student Teacher in Salford 1959-60; Mature student Manchester University 1960-65; Lecturer in Public Administration, Salford University 1965-70; President University of Manchester Union 1963-64; Author of *Industrial Manager, Colne Valley: Radicalism to Socialism, Victor Grayson: Labour's Lost Leader.* Unsuccessfully contested the Withington division of Manchester in 1966. Elected for Colne Valley division of the West Riding of Yorkshire in June 1970 and sat until February 1974 when he was defeated. Unsuccessfully contested Colne Valley in October 1974. Elected for South Shields in May 1979. Opposition spokesman on Agriculture and Food 1972-74; Defence 1980-81; Environment 1981-86; Shadow Cabinet 1986-92 covering Environmental Protection; Food and Agriculture.

William Blyton *MP Houghton-le-Spring 1945-64*
Son of Charles H Blyton, of South Shields. Born 2 May 1899; married 26 December 1919, Jane. Educated at Elementary School. Served in Royal Navy 1916-18. Miner 1914-45. Official of Harton Miners' Executive Committee 1930-31; 1932-33 and 1942-43. Member of South Shields Town Council 1936-45; Parliamentary Private Secretary to G S Lindgren Parliamentary Secretary Ministry of Civil Aviation 1947-May 1949. Delegate to Council of Europe, Strasbourg 1949, 1950 and 1951. Created Baron Blyton (Life Peerage) 1964. Died 25 October 1987.

Richard Ewart *MP Sunderland 1945-50, Sunderland South 1950-53*
Son of Richard Ewart. Born 15 September 1904. Unmarried. Educated at St Bede's, South Shields. Organiser for the National Union of General and Municipal Workers. Member of South Shields Borough Council 1932-43, and of North Riding of Yorkshire County Council 1943-53. Parliamentary Private Secretary to Sir Hartley Shawcross, President of the Board of Trade 1951. A Roman Catholic. Died 8 March 1953.

Joyce Quin *MEP Tyne and Wear 1979-89; MP Gateshead East 1987-*
Daughter of Basil Godfrey Quin and Ida (nee Ritson). Born Tynemouth, 26 November 1944.   Unmarried. Educated at Monkseaton Junior and Whitley Bay Grammar Schools, Newcastle University (BA Hons French - 1st Class) and London University. Research Assistant at Labour Party HQ 1969-72.   Lecturer in French at University of Bath 1972-76 and at University of Durham 1977-79. Opposition front bench spokesperson on trade and industry, 1989-.   Member of Select Committee on Treasury and Civil Service, 1987-89. Hon Fellow, Sunderland Polytechnic, 1986.   Publications: various articles in newspapers and journals.

Alan Donnelly *MEP Tyne and Wear 1989-*
Son of John and Josephine Donnelly. Born 16 July 1957. Educated Springfield Comprehensive School, Sunderland Polytechnic.   CLP Secretary for Jarrow 1976-81. Parliamentary Agent to Don Dixon MP in 1979 General Election.   Regional Education Officer GMB 1978-83, Regional Finance and Administrative Officer and Press Liaison Officer for Regional Secretary of Northern GMB 1983-87.   National Finance Director for GMB 1987-89. Director, Unity Trust Bank 1987-89.   Member, South Tyneside Council 1980-84.

APPENDIX F

THE GENERAL COMMITTEE 1992

Organisation	Name
All Saints	Joyce Harper
	Betty Dryden
	Ethel Lamb
	Jim Harper
Beacon & Bents	Nancy Gladstone
	Steve Hamilton
	Margaret Tarn
	Katharine Tarn
	Sheila Guthrie
	Audrey McMillan
Cleadon Park	Jim Moore
	Hazel Grey
	Brian Buckley
Harton	Linda Edwardson
	Robert Edwardson
	Edward Killen
	Brian Storey
Horsley Hill	Mark Walsh
	Neil Maxwell
	Cathy Brown
	Fred Davies
Rekendyke	John Turner
	John Turner Jr
	Stuart Dunleavy
	Richard Hughes
	Mohamed Hussein
Tyne Dock & Simonside	Margaret Massingham
	Amelia McLean
	Frank Mills
	Michael Clare

Westoe

Jane Branley
Allen Branley
Ron Reynolds
Audrey Carter
Margaret Hamilton

West Park

Graeme Keedy
Robert Watters
Sheila Emmett
Pauline Jackson
Don Taylor

Whiteleas

Robert Emmerson
J Terry Haram
Jack Taylor
Albert Elliott
Frank Coverdale

Women's Section

Shirley Stratford
Cecilia Pearson

LPYS

Fabians

Irene Thornton

Co-op

Arthur Jackson
Lilian Jordison
Ken Webster
Joan Jackson

GMB
S/S 1 (Boilermakers)

Bob Stidolph

S/S 2 (Boilermakers)

Ronnie Johnson

S/S 3 (Boilermakers)

Alex Greig
Tommy Brennan
Bill Coates

S/S 1

Ivor Richardson

S/S 2	Warren Turnbull Tony Winter Iain Malcolm Norma Winter Gerry Graham
S/S General	Syed Hussain
S/T General	John Johnson David Urwin Derek Chandler Margaret Haram
S/T LA	Andy Frost Paul Harrison Pat Tate John Temple Sheila Temple
N/C/C Holding	Elsie Stidolph John Bargh
Ryhope	Albert Tate
Sunderland 10	Ronnie Lumsdale
AEU	Bob Robertson
COHSE	Bob Haws
EETPU (Plumbers) (Electricians)	Bill Brady Arthur Fox
MSF	Joe McAlroy
NUM Miners Lodge (Westoe)	Edward Malcolm Bob Coates Norman Blenkinsop Bill Lilley David Kenrick

NUPE (Health)   Velda McMillan
Bill McDonald
Joe Humphrey
Beryl Scott

NUPE (LA)   Brian Steele
Evelyn Doneghan
Jim Doneghan
Maureen Gallagher

RMT   Joe Piggot
Said Salem

TGWU 8/42   Jimmy Thompson
Jim Foreman
Stephen Forster

USDAW   Peter Brook

INDEX